Religion, State, and Political Culture in Japan

CRITICAL PERSPECTIVES ON RELIGION IN INTERNATIONAL POLITICS

Series Editors: Giorgio Shani and Mustapha Pasha

In recent years, the discipline of International Relations has undergone a religious renaissance. The distinction between the religious and the secular has been brought into question by a resurgence of interest in religion, culture, and identity in the context of international politics, forcing mainstream theories to take religion seriously. Furthermore, efforts to "provincialize" IR by bringing in voices from "outside" the West have stimulated interest in other religious traditions that have hitherto been marginalized in the discipline. Attempts have also been made to free IR from its dominant secular orientation through an encounter with the "post-secular," which can open up productive avenues of inquiry. The overall objective of this series, therefore, is to open up space for critical scholarship on Religion and International Relations and to "post-secular" approaches to global politics. The main aims of the series are to decenter and pluralize discussions of religion in international politics by bringing into question the theological underpinnings of IR and by creating room for the articulation of alternative understandings of the relationship between the "religious" and "political" from other faith traditions.

Titles in the Series

The Refugee Crisis and Religion: Secularism, Security and Hospitality in Question edited by Luca Mavelli and Erin Wilson

Faith-Based Organizations in Transnational Peacebuilding by Tanya B. Schwarz

Rethinking Peace: Discourse, Memory, Translation, and Dialogue edited by Alexander Laban Hinton, Giorgio Shani, and Jeremiah Alberg

Beyond Modernity: Critical Perspectives on Islam, Tradition and Power edited by Emi Goto and Mohammed Moussa

Religion, State, and Political Culture in Japan: Implications for the Post-Secular World by Tokihisa Sumimoto

Religion, State, and Political Culture in Japan

Implications for the Post-Secular World

Tokihisa Sumimoto

ROWMAN & LITTLEFIELD
Lanham • Boulder • New York • London

Published by Rowman & Littlefield
An imprint of The Rowman & Littlefield Publishing Group, Inc.
4501 Forbes Boulevard, Suite 200, Lanham, Maryland 20706
www.rowman.com

86-90 Paul Street, London EC2A 4NE

British Library Cataloguing in Publication Information Available

Library of Congress Cataloging-in-Publication Data

Includes bibliographic references and index.
ISBN: 978-1-78660-594-8 (cloth)
ISBN: 978-1-78660-595-5 (electronic)

∞™ The paper used in this publication meets the minimum requirements of American National Standard for Information Sciences—Permanence of Paper for Printed Library Materials, ANSI/NISO Z39.48-1992.

To Yuko, Hisashi, and Yuri

Contents

Preface and Acknowledgments

A new world order in the post-Cold War and post-secular era has been a major topic of argument by many scholars of international affairs, such as Glen Fukushima and Samuel Huntington. The 9/11 incident, which occurred amid these arguments, made it clear that a conventional national-security approach alone is incapable of coping with the new situations caused by aggressive nonstate actors with nonconventional motivations. Globally, the increasing dominance of the logic of geopolitics and market economy has contributed to widening economic gaps between and within countries, as well as to the emergence of religious extremism. Tension between the secular and the religious, which had once been considered settled with the Westphalian arrangement, has reemerged as a global issue. At the same time, traditional power competition and tension between states and between blocs are only increasing, as highlighted by the ongoing Russia-Ukraine war. Finland's decision to join the North Atlantic Treaty Organization in April 2023 after maintaining decades of military neutrality was perhaps an inevitable move for the country, but it also increases tension and the risk of a direct collision between the Western alliance and Russia. Under these circumstances of political turmoil and uncertainty, no obvious solution is available. We must, nevertheless, continue to pursue ways to achieve peace and to democratize and humanize the world. This book is written with the aim to contribute to these causes.

This book arises out of conversations with Georgio Shani, the editor of Rowman & Littlefield's Religion and International Relations series, who first suggested that I write this book and has since provided consistent encouragement. Jim Whitman, the general editor of Palgrave

Macmillan's Global Issues series, reviewed the manuscript and made insightful and detailed comments and suggestions, which led to significant improvements in both its substance and organization. Throughout the writing of this book, Lily Renfro, an alumna of Columbia University, provided indispensable editorial work and substantive advice. Ashley Dodge and Laney Ackley at Rowman & Littlefield, with patience and unwavering support, have professionally guided the manuscript through the publication process. I am immensely grateful to these individuals for their help in bringing this book into being. At the same time, I would like to thank my mentors for their encouragement and to thank my family, to whom this book is also dedicated, for their love and support.

Note for Readers

Romanization of Japanese terms follows the Hepburn system, and Japanese names are written with the surname first, followed by the personal name, except in some direct quotes.

Introduction

Political ideology and religious faith often demonstrate similarities in both character and outcomes, often seeking to expand their social influence domestically as well as globally. At the same time, religion differs from politics in that it is transcendental in origin, a fact that contributes to the historical tensions between secular authority and religious authority.[1] Western European countries addressed this tension and ended their own religious wars by establishing states grounded in secularism.[2] In the Soviet Union, attempts were made to eliminate this tension through an extreme variant of secularism, the antireligious atheism that Marxism/Leninism entails. However, this could not eradicate or even substantially reduce the social influence of the Russian Orthodox Church, as will be further discussed in chapter 2. Further, it is of interest to note that the kind of fervor associated with Marxism/Leninism has been often described as "secular religion."[3] Elsewhere, one of the major non-Western approaches to addressing this tension has been the establishment of Sharia law, which essentially erases the lines between divine and secular by reconciling religious belief and secular authority. In practice, nevertheless, tensions remain, including around the question of who interprets the words of God, politicizing what is originally transcendental in nature. In the case of Japan, however, religion as a set of universal values transcending local politics never attained a status by which it might compete with secular government. Prior to the modern time, power holders, such as the feudal military governments, openly wielded religion as a tool for managing and subduing Japan's people. In the country's modern period leading to World War II, Japan's imperial rule formed a state religion expressly designed to extend the emperor's authority over his subjects. The end of the war marked the beginning of a new dawn for Japan after the promulgation of the new constitution, which brought about genuine religious freedom. Nevertheless, contemporary Japan has remained in a spiritual vacuum due to the country's state-centric culture and the sway of religious factions.

CONTEMPORARY JAPAN'S SPIRITUAL VACUUM

Japan exhibits great religious apathy, as the majority of the people lack serious observance of any given religion due to the decline of Buddhism, Shinto, and Christianity in Japanese society. According to statistics from NHK, the country's public broadcaster, over 60 percent of the Japanese population does not follow a particular religion.[4] The lack of knowledge about religion among the Japanese implies that Japan lacks great interest in religious doctrine. That being said, some Shinto shrines have survived by offering visits on New Year's Day and conducting weddings, implying that ritual observance is still a common practice. Similarly, Buddhist temples play a role by offering funeral services and graveyards. These activities, however, only serve local transactional and practical needs for rituals rather than encouraging a broader spiritual perspective bolstered by religious doctrine.

There is a longstanding Westphalian consensus that political virtues emerge as a modern secular state leaves religion behind. However, in the case of Japan, this book argues, these virtues have not been fully developed partly due to the absence of grassroots perspectives nourished with spirituality and religiosity. This argument aligns with Richard Falk's view that the failure of today's secular thinking is partly attributable to the "exclusion of religious and spiritual dimensions of human experience from the shaping of the vision and practices associated with the quest for global humane governance."[5]

THE VALUE OF RELIGION FOR SECULAR SOCIETY AND THE THEORETICAL FRAMEWORK

The post-Westphalian world order tends to consider secularism, rather than religiosity, as more conducive to free and democratic governance.

It is under this prevailing world order that globalization has taken place on an unprecedented scale. Technological innovations have expedited globalization, but this has also caused many problems, such as expanding economic gaps both between countries and within countries. Additionally, the recent occurrence of the COVID-19 pandemic has only exacerbated these issues. Other modern problems that governments must work together to combat include climate change and terrorism.

Globalization to this point has been led by market and geopolitical forces where democratic and humane governance is lacking. Though there are some voices representing civil societies, including nongovernmental organizations, expressing their views through the United Nations system; the influence of these groups on actual policy is limited. Thus, an alternate approach to addressing these problems on a national and international scale should be considered.

In the field of international studies, Falk proposes a perspective of "reconstructive postmodernism," which he defines as a "post-Westphalian perspective that is informed by ethical values and spiritual belief," as a possible solution to these global issues by making the world more humane and democratic.[6] He argues that the "positive inclusive tendencies in secularism and religious outlooks need to bond, without subverting their distinctive forms of attentiveness to human suffering and aspiration, in the course of defining 'humane globalization,'" emphasizing his view in favor of collaboration and reconciliation.[7]

This book draws on the concept of reconstructive postmodernism as a theoretical framework for analyzing the various problems of Japan and suggesting solutions. I had an opportunity to discuss this approach with Falk via email when I started working on my PhD dissertation, on which this book is partly based. In his email to me, Falk said, "I am delighted that you will pursue work on the relevance of religious perspectives to Japanese political culture. I think your assessment of the problematics of Japan as a result of extreme militarist phase followed by an economistic phase is very perceptive."[8]

Thus, it is one of the arguments of this book that contemporary Japanese politics would benefit from a "post-secular" openness to a religious perspective. The universality of religious tradition would help Japan in regard to human rights, leading to the development of a civil society that is influential enough to help shape government policies.

The concept of religiosity for this book's argument involves the notion of universality and transcendence. A universal and transcendent religion is depicted as a doctrine and practice understood as linked to a morality inherent in all humans, to a beneficent universe and/or divinity, while extending beyond local power-holder interests or partisan politics. Therefore, a religious perspective means a perspective far enough outside politics to be able to offer criticism of it but not so far outside that religion becomes simply abstract and strictly private.

I derive the universal and transcendent nature of the religious perspective in part from Falk's argument about the relationship between religious values and democratic politics. Falk criticizes the cost-benefit calculative nature of much global governance in today's world, describing it as "global inhumane governance."[9] He calls for the "role of religion as a way of . . . 'humanizing' globalization by the advocacy of a global ethic"[10] while recognizing the "double-edged relevance of religion,"[11] the negative side of which refers to religious extremism and the opportunistic use of religion by power holders.

In response to examples of religious authority invoked for legitimizing the act of war, Falk suggests a format for more positive contributions to be made by religion. If organized religion is to achieve spiritual authority, it must respond independently to state power, unwavering in its commitment to peacefulness and justice and dedicated to the pursuit of spiritual goals in both public and private spaces. These spiritual goals need to accord with widely endorsed ethical goals such as the avoidance of war, the mitigation of poverty, struggles against oppression, and campaigns to restore and maintain nature and safeguard the sanctity of life.[12]

As this suggests, although religion may sometimes sink into narrow or biased views, in general, we are to use it to strive for broadly understood notions of good, coming as close to universal as possible.

For Falk, these universal goals ideally help religious perspectives transcend partisan politics and fixed identities. Falk provides a rationale for his emphasis on the role of religion, stating that "the religious awakening can contribute to the formation of identities that . . . can foster from positions of deep rootedness an understanding and celebration of a transcendent common humanity."[13] To counterbalance global governance centered on geopolitics and market forces, which the United Nations tries and fails to achieve, Falk calls for religion's contribution: "The religious challenge is to infuse the struggle of the peoples of the world for democracy, equity, and sustainability with a vision of human existence that is human-centered yet conscious of the relevance of the sacred and of mysteries beyond the grasp of reason and machines."[14]

Nevertheless, no naive concept of religion is intended here, because religions can operate, and have operated, to support corrupt politics. At worst, religion can sow conflict by encouraging notions of superiority. As Falk notes:

> It is evident that religion cannot be reduced to any single religious tradition, although it can draw strength from the collaborative support of the various traditions, and that some aspects of certain religious traditions are antithetical, especially claims of being "the chosen people" or the exclusive or superior instruments of a divine or sacred design or of the enactment of some apocalyptic scenario for ascent to a higher form of existence.[15]

Despite these risks, the present text argues that religion has a better chance than other social institutions of imbuing Japanese politics with a sense of democratic values. This book endorses the view that modern democracy and the attendant values of human rights and equal treatment should be nurtured with religious values. In Falk's words, "It is time that the post-Enlightenment divide between religion and politics [be] drawn into question so that the great legal texts of human rights can receive a civilizational and societal ratification as well as a formal acceptance at the level of government."[16]

Witte and Green also argue that religious ideas play a key role in creating a conducive environment for human rights to survive.[17] Therefore, human rights and equal treatment naturally coincide with religious transcendence.

SCHOLARSHIP ON JAPANESE RELIGION

Previous historical studies have tended to have a somewhat negative view of the role of religion in modern Japan. These studies often note the destructive effects of the military authorities' manipulative use of Shinto during World War II. Helen Hardacre has recently discussed the stalemate in scholarship between those who hold a totalizing view of State Shinto, as if "a blueprint had already existed in 1868 for everything that would unfold through 1945," and those who undertake "hyper-detailed parsing of government documents and ideological distinctions aiming to 'whitewash' Shinto."[18] Although the present text uses the term "State Shinto" to describe the government's program of propaganda, it is not ultimately interested in determining how culpable Shinto was for Japan's military imperialism nor in exploring the details of Shinto as a religion per se. Instead, this book argues that State Shinto was invented by the prewar government to fuel the development of nationalism and ultimately militarism. This has contributed to skepticism about religion in Japan after World War II.

The present text thus differs from previous studies by telling the story of religion in Japan in a way that tries to account for the nation's present-day spiritual vacuum and imperfect democratic politics. Arguably, the religious freedom of modern secularism often amounts to neutralizing the public force of religion by shunting it into the private. In contrast, this book calls for a post-secular religious tolerance in which the state opens itself to guidance and critique from a religious perspective, even when it finds this perspective politically inconvenient.

Moreover, as Aizawa Hisashi points out, there have been relatively few studies conducted on Japanese religions from the perspective of social science as opposed to those from the perspective of religious studies per se in humanities.[19] Aizawa's observation remains valid today. This book, therefore, also contributes to this space needing more scholarship.

STRUCTURE OF THE BOOK

This book consists of six chapters. The first two chapters will provide global context by reviewing and analyzing various paradigms with respect to the relationship between the state and religion or religious institutions. The first chapter focuses on regional and country-specific paradigms where secularization and modernization has developed, though in varying forms. The second chapter presents case studies on foreign and domestic policy issues of major countries involving religious institutions and state authorities. These paradigms and case studies provide perspectives on Japan-specific discussions being made in the third chapter onward.

The third chapter will begin by reviewing the historical backdrop for Japan's religion-state relations with a focus on national unifiers and the feudal military government in the early modern period. It will show the government authorities' intolerance toward religious authorities and movements. The same chapter will then examine religion-state relations in the modern period. Against the secular backdrop developed by the preceding period's power holders, as will be argued, the modern period's state authorities created a religion of state worship to foster nationalism, seeking to be competitive against foreign powers. Eventually, Japan's nationalism, combined with the artificial religion of state worship, developed into ultranationalism and militarism, driving the country to aggression against other Asian countries and into World War II.

The fourth chapter will examine the militarist authorities' ideology with a focus on the government publication *Kokutai no hongi* (Fundamental Principles of the National Structure).[20] This examination will demonstrate the government's emphasis on state/emperor worship and the explicit rejection of democratic values. The same chapter will introduce the contrasting ideas of Makiguchi Tsunesaburō, who was among the few religious figures in the modern period with an uncompromising stance against the ideology of, and persecution by, the militarist government.

The fifth chapter will analyze political reforms implemented in Japan by the Allied Powers's occupation authorities at the end of World War II, with the emphasis of these reforms on religious policy. The chapter will show that these political reforms transformed Japan from an autocracy based on the rule of man into a democracy based on the rule of law, in part by prohibiting state interference in religious beliefs and practices. At the same time, the chapter will argue that the constitutional and institutional reforms alone could not fundamentally change Japan's political culture, which had developed over centuries. It will describe a religious vacuum seen in Japan after World War II despite the robust guarantee of freedom of religion provided by the new constitution.

The sixth chapter will examine how new and conventional religions in Japan have responded to this postwar environment. The chapter will show that most religions have remained socially and politically uninfluential because they are unable to appeal to a substantial segment of the country's population. There are some major exceptions to this rule, which this chapter will discuss. It will use as an example the lay Buddhist group, Sōka Gakkai, providing a perspective on its political and social influence. The chapter will also show the attempted revival of religious control by state authorities. It will argue that such attempts reflect Japan's political culture, mirrored by the underdevelopment of democratic values including the rule of law, human rights, and civil society. Furthermore, the same chapter will consider global implications of the case of Japan in terms of relations between religion and state. Underdevelopment of the democratic political culture in Japan is to a noteworthy degree attributable to the lack of religious and philosophical tradition guided by transcendent ethical values. In Falk's relevant words referring to the problematic aspects of globalization, "the political leverage of [grassroots] forces is likely to remain limited . . . unless such dispositions are strengthened by religious commitments and by support of the organized religious community."[21] In the past, autonomous religious movements in Japan were either destroyed by state authorities or neutralized by being incorporated into the power structure. Today, the same challenge faces religious movements seeking a sociopolitical influence in the country. A broad implication is that developing human-centric global governance necessitates meaningful dialogues and collaborations among religious traditions and between the religious and the secular. The chapter will argue that the state-centric nature of the modern world can to some extent be attributed to a lack of religious aspiration shared among different traditions to establish ethical values that are independent of political and economic interests. The chapter will also consider and suggest potential solutions to the problematics.

NOTES

1. Nakano Minoru, *Shūkyō to seiji* [Religion and politics] (Tokyo: Shinhyoron Publishing, 1998), 25–35.

2. Richard Falk, *Religion and Humane Global Governance* (New York: Palgrave, 2001), 39.

3. Anatoly M. Khazanov, "Marxism-Leninism as a Secular Religion," in *The Sacred in Twentieth-Century Politics*, ed. Roger Griffin, Robert Mallett, and

John Tortorice (London: Palgrave Macmillan, 2008), 119–20, https://doi.org/10.1057/9780230241633_7 (May 2, 2023).

4. Kobayashi Toshiyuki, "Nihonjin no shūkyōteki ishiki ya kōdō wa dō kawattaka" [How have the Japanese people's religious awareness and behaviors changed?], *Hōsōkekyū to chōsa* [Broadcasting Research and Surveys], April 2019: 53.

5. Falk, *Religion*, 16.

6. Falk, *Religion*, 11.

7. Falk, *Religion*, 10.

8. Richard Falk, email message to author, March 19, 2002.

9. Falk, *Religion*, 17.

10. Falk, *Religion*, 75.

11. Falk, *Religion*, 16.

12. Falk, *Religion*, 114.

13. Falk, *Religion*, 8.

14. Falk, *Religion*, 33.

15. Falk, *Religion*, 29.

16. Falk, *Religion*, 8.

17. J. Witte Jr. and M. C. Green, eds., *Religion and Human Rights: An Introduction* (New York: Oxford University Press, 2011).

18. Helen Hardacre, *Shinto: A History* (New York: Oxford University Press, 2017), 356–57.

19. Aizawa Hisashi, *Gendai kokka ni okeru shūkyō to seiji* [Religion and politics in contemporary states] (Tokyo: Keiso Shobo, 1966).

20. There is a range of English translations of the title of *Kokutai no hongi.* The English title used in this book, unless stated otherwise, follows the official translation appearing in the Shinto Directive issued by the Supreme Commander of the Allied Powers during the postwar occupation period, which will be discussed in the fifth chapter.

21. Falk, *Religion*, 25.

Chapter 1

The Enduring Tensions Between Organized Religions and the State

Case Studies in Secularization and Modernization

This chapter creates and provides a comparative and international perspective, using region- and country-specific paradigms, before proceeding to the discussions on religion and state relationships in Japan in chapter 3 and onward. Religious wars in Europe from the sixteenth to the seventeenth century, culminating in the Thirty Years' War, triggered the region's states to conclude that they should be neutral with respect to religion, though situations varied by country. In this post-Westphalian context, the first four cases illustrate the varying church and state relationships in Western Europe, the United Kingdom, Russia, and the United States. The fifth case focuses on North Korea coopting quasi-theocratic ideology. The last section of this chapter discusses the case of India and its experience of religious violence and undue religious influence on the state despite the country's constitutional guarantee of religious freedom.

WESTERN EUROPE AND THE CHURCH: THE PLACE OF RELIGION IN PREMODERN EUROPE

Europe's religious transformation provides a perspective on religion and state relationships in Japan versus in Western countries. The place of religion in state politics has always been a controversial topic, especially in the premodern period. Before Christianity was introduced in many nations, political and religious order was not well defined in those civilizations. Dennis Mueller provided a well-documented and researched history in his 2013 article "The State and Religion."[1] The scholar contended that, in the case of the Roman Empire, the emperor was a living god, and the state was run by an elite class including a cadre of priests. As such, religion was nothing more than a branch of the state. This relationship changed once Christianity became the state religion of Rome. In the course of its first eight centuries, the Church saw its mission as extending to all nations, not just Rome. The first century AD was dominated by pagan rulers, especially in Europe. Christian apostles taught their disciples to obey the governing body as long as obedience to the state did not violate their divine law.[2] In Europe, the emphasis on the primacy of spirituality became stronger among Christian theologians during the first century AD. During this time, Christianity had become a religion of the empire.[3] Civil authority fell under the leadership of the educated few, most of whom were churchmen, during the end of the Roman Empire. Soon, the Church, headquartered in Constantinople, became virtually the only spiritual and temporal power in Europe.

The secular kings had regained power throughout Europe by 800 AD, and the power struggle between the Church and secular leaders heightened in the tenth century. In his 2011 book *The Medieval Church: From the Dawn of the Middle Ages to the Eve of the Reformation*, Carl A. Volz argues that the Church was involved in constant conflicts with feudal lords, with whom it wanted to maintain good relations.[4] Corruption in the Church was also high as Church leaders began practicing simony (the practice of selling ecclesiastical offices to rich people and the highest bidders) instead of working with people who were educated and trained to follow the ways of the Church.[5] Additionally, many priests and monks did not attend schools, which meant that they exercised power despite being unable to actually read the sacred texts themselves.[6] Further, many monks and priests failed to live by their vows of honesty and chastity.

A reform movement would soon develop in the early tenth century that saw the implementation of stricter rules for monks and priests. Priests and abbots were also appointed to manage ecclesiastical offices. In *The Oxford History of Medieval Europe*, George Holmes discusses the medieval period and argues that the Papal Reform Movement also emerged during this time.[7] The establishment of the monastery at Cluny saw the first wave of reform in 910.[8] Monks were taken to school and educated about their sacred roles and responsibilities based on strict rules. A third wave came when the secular lords began challenging the papal leadership. A struggle between the emperor and the pope emerged because the pope sought absolute control and took away the power of the secular lords to control ecclesiastical offices or select their leaders. Secular rulers did not take this well, and a conflict emerged that challenged the origin of a ruler's power.[9] The secular lords believed power came from citizens, while the Church believed that power originated from God.

The climax of the conflict occurred when Henry IV and Pope Gregory VI engaged in a propaganda war by distributing pamphlets that explained the origin of power. The pope argued that he had temporal rule over secular leaders and was at liberty to withdraw the privileges the kings and lords enjoyed whenever they went against the temporal rule. By the 1070s, the heated nature of the conflict led to the excommunication of Henry IV by Pope Gregory VI. Henry IV would soon admit defeat in 1077, but the damage was already done, and the power struggle continued for years as kings tried to redefine the governing power and the right to sovereignty.[10] Regardless of the details of these disputes, it was clear that the Church wanted to gain power. Volz provides insight that this was illustrated when the Church started the Crusades that campaigned against Islam to take back the holy lands from Islamic control. Internal political affairs also affected the Church, which led to the split between the Western and Eastern Church that resulted in the Catholic Church and the Eastern Orthodox Church.[11]

Papal power increased immensely in the twelfth and thirteenth centuries as the Church sought more power. The pope implemented decrees that were obeyed more than those of secular kings. By 1500, the heightened conflict had led to major political and religious changes. Martin

Luther analyzed the situation and was frustrated by church practices like the issuing of indulgences. As such, he moved on and established a Protestant movement. He called for an open debate, resulting in the separation of the whole of Europe into the Catholic south and Protestant north. The conflict was heightened in the fourteenth century by the emergence of nationalism.[12] This was a period when papal authority experienced a great deal of pressure from secular leaders. For instance, Queen Elizabeth I separated the Church of England from papal authority, which led to her excommunication.

It is clear that the Christian Church appealed to universal authority to both compete and interact with state powers. In fact, the war between the Protestants and Roman Catholics split Europe into many ideological factions. Kings and princes selected the religion that they wanted for their people, and their citizens were expected to abide by their command. By the fifteenth century, as Henry Kamen discusses in his 2000 book *Early Modern European Society*, the reforms and ambitions of princes and kings led to the advancement of the state church in most European countries. The new institutions were publicly supported and sanctioned. People were expected to worship in these geographical units, and every person was expected to worship in the main parish church.[13]

Europe from the mid-sixteenth to the mid-seventeenth centuries was battered by the Thirty Years' War and the Eighty Years' War, both deadly, prolonged religious wars. The Peace of Westphalia, a set of treaties signed in 1648, brought the religious wars in Europe to an end. The treaties are generally regarded as the starting point of the modern, that is, secular state system. The state accepted the legal obligation to protect religious freedom domestically and not to make war against other states to impose a particular religion, making the treaties a milestone toward the secularization of these European countries. The processes and outcomes of secularization, nevertheless, varied from country to country, making generalizations misleading.[14]

FROM THE PAPACY TO THE CHURCH OF ENGLAND: THE CASE OF THE UNITED KINGDOM, A CONSTITUTIONAL MONARCHY

The development of church-state relations in the United Kingdom differs from that in continental Europe, where after the Reformation and the signing of the Peace of Westphalia, the basic direction was to secularize the state. The English Reformation, in contrast, was preceded by the kingdom's split from the papacy and the Church of England's break from the Roman Catholic Church. The Church of England, however, initially remained Catholic in theology and rituals. Though it became Protestant later, the basic structural integration of church and state has remained unchanged until today without intentional secularization of the state. On the other hand, however, the country is seeing an increasing trend of secular thinking among its people. This section briefly reviews the United Kingdom's history of church and state relations and then touches upon the emergence of a secularistic generation, a factor necessitating the kingdom's rethinking of its future religious policy.

Prior to the Reformation that brought about the Protestant-Catholic divide, kingdoms were referred to as fiefs of the papacy, which means that they were under the control and influence of the popes. This arrangement began in England when King John surrendered his kingdom to the papacy in 1213, receiving it back as a vassal rendering an annual tribute.[15] King Henry VIII, however, broke this quid pro quo arrangement when he divorced his wife, Catherine of Aragon, and married his second wife, Anne Boleyn, in secret after unsuccessfully seeking an annulment from the Catholic Church. This led to him being excommunicated from the Church for going against its doctrines, infuriating King Henry VIII, and leading him to push through with the Act of Supremacy. This act gave him and all his heirs the title of Supreme Head of the Church of England, depriving the pope of his religious authority in England.[16] Thus, England's initial break from papal authority was more due to King Henry VIII's personal motives. This is in contrast to the case of Protestant reform movements in continental Europe, which were spurred by criticism of the corruption of the Catholic Church and of its rituals that hampered relations between individuals and God.[17]

The Parliament's official passage of the Act of Supremacy in 1534 solidified the break from the Catholic Church. Known as the

English Reformation, this process confirmed that the king had legal sovereignty of the civil laws over and above the laws of the Catholic Church; the king could select bishops and all other religious leaders in the empire and had power over them. Under Protestant-educated Edward IV, who held the throne from 1547 to 1553, the English Reformation increased in its theological and social significance. It became "much more than political: it felt personal since it cut so deeply into people's habits and beliefs."[18] Though Rome's jurisdiction was temporarily restored in 1553 under Queen Mary I; this was soon reversed in 1558 under Queen Elizabeth I, who became supreme governor of the Church of England in 1559. The Parliament passed the second Act of Supremacy of 1558, which further solidified England's separation from the papal authority. The act required all clergy, judges, and other civil officials to make an oath denying the supremacy of the pope. Anyone who refused to take the oath was dismissed from his/her position.[19] The first Elizabethan Archbishop of Canterbury was appointed in December 1559 and has since remained the "Primate of all England" (that is, the first bishop) except from 1646 to 1660 when episcopacy was suspended by Parliament until it was restored by King Charles II.[20] The supreme governor of the Church of England is the British monarch, and the Church of England is an "established" church in the United Kingdom, meaning that it is directly involved in various government activities.[21]

The constitutional links between the government and the Church of England are deeply rooted. The British monarch appoints Church of England bishops on the advice of the prime minister based on a list of candidates proposed by the Church; there are also twenty-six places reserved for the most senior bishops of the Church of England in the House of Lords. The Church of Scotland is also an established church but with a lesser level of political involvement, having no representation in the parliament. While the British monarch is supreme governor of the Church of England, he or she is only a "member" of the Church of Scotland, sending a representative to the church's general assembly.

The close relationship between the church and the monarch in the United Kingdom continues to represent complex church-state relations as well as the kingdom's internal power balances, which face external challenges such as an increasing inflow of immigrants with different religious backgrounds as well as the rise of secular thinking among its people. A 2018 survey showed that 52 percent of the respondents in

England and Wales said they are nonreligious, growing from 43 percent a decade before. The survey found the change largely attributable to generational change; only 1 percent of those aged eighteen to twenty-four said they belong to the Church of England, compared to 33 percent of those aged seventy-five and above, with the percentages declining in relation to the age groups.[22] Another survey conducted in 2021 indicated that 41 percent of the respondents aged eighteen to twenty-four believed that there should now be an elected head of state compared to 31 percent who preferred a king or queen. This result showed a reversal of sentiment from 2019, when 46 percent supported the monarchy compared to 26 percent who wanted it replaced.[23] In the past, Protestantism and anti-Catholic sentiment played a significant role in raising "an awareness of the religious unity of Britain."[24] However, with the people's religious sentiment declining and their perceptions toward the monarchy changing, the United Kingdom's constitutional monarchy with its sovereign as the supreme governor of the Church of England as a system unifying the kingdom seems to be subject to reexamination in the future.

THE CONFLICT BETWEEN ORTHODOX CHRISTIANITY AND THE ATHEIST USSR DURING ITS PERIOD OF SECULARIZATION AND MODERNIZATION

Before the Russian Revolution, especially from the seventeenth century, the Russian Orthodox Church enjoyed a privileged status in helping the Russian Empire consolidate the nation. In return, the Church was placed under the imperial system's control as the state church with the tsar officially appointed as its head. Religious education was compulsory at all schools. Certificates of birth, marriage, and death were issued by the Church.[25] In these and other ways, the Russian Orthodox Church was omnipresent in daily life.[26]

The Russian Revolution that commenced in 1917 marked a turning point not only in the economic sphere but also in the relationship between the Russian Orthodox Church and the state. The Soviet authority began pursuing modernization and economic growth with centrally planned socialism.[27] This pursuit was coupled with forced secularization. Replacing religious belief with scientific atheism, the official belief system of the Soviet Communist Party, was considered imperative by the state power holders.[28] With the goal of establishing state atheism, the USSR employed massive state resources to eradicate the religious beliefs of the Russian Orthodox Church and other churches, or "prerevolutionary remnants."[29] In its six decades of rule, however, the communist regime saw the persistence of its people's religious commitment and proved "unsuccessful in severing masses of Soviet citizens from their religious identities."[30] Furthermore, facing external challenges during World War II, the regime had to significantly soften its policy toward the churches and even seek their help in supporting the state defense efforts, as will be examined later shortly.

Soon after the Bolsheviks came into power, they commenced initiatives to implement official forced atheization, including introducing legislation against the Russian Orthodox Church and other churches. The Decree on Separation of Church and State of January 23, 1918, declared all churches dissociated from the state and from the educational system. It also deprived the churches of the right to hold property. While the legislation did not specify a particular church, the resulting effect was the most devastating on the wealth and privileges of the Russian Orthodox Church given its prerevolution status.[31]

The Soviet government's antireligious outlook stemmed from the ideology and practice associated with Marxism-Leninism. This is symbolically indicated by Marx's strictures against religion as the opiate of the people and the ultra-empirical embrace of atheism, a doctrine based on the idea that what cannot be verified by scientific examination as falsifiable does not exist. Ironically, communist atheism had to employ a religious character to strengthen its appeal to the people, including by venerating Lenin with "chapels set aside and statutes of the departed leader illuminated by soft light or even by candles."[32]

The Soviet authority's antireligious stance was increasingly strengthened in the 1920s and 1930s, including through more legislative actions. Previously, the Constitution of the Russian Federated Socialist Republic of July 10, 1918, stipulated in Article 13: "For the purpose of securing to the workers real freedom of conscience, the church is separated from the state and the school from the church, and the right of religious and anti-religious propaganda is accorded to every citizen." However, the Constitution was later modified in 1929, and the words mentioning the right of religious propaganda were removed, leaving only the words mentioning the right of antireligious propaganda and separation of the church from the state in the article. Furthermore, a symptomatic legislative move was the enactment of the Laws on Religious Association of 1929. The laws required every religious association to register with local Soviet authorities. In practice, according to Edward Derwinski's witness appearing in a House of Representatives report, the state used the laws to "limit the number of religious associations, to reduce their number gradually, and even to deny legal status to an entire religious denomination."[33]

The Great Purge, Joseph Stalin's campaign to remove political rivals that occurred from 1936 to 1938, caused devastating damage to the Russian Orthodox Church, closing down over 10,000 eparchies.[34] By 1939, only approximately 2,000 churches remained open, compared to some 46,000 before the revolution.[35] Despite this, however, the public's "loyalty to the virtually nonexistent church remained substantial."[36]

When Nazi-led Germany invaded the USSR in June 1941, breaking the Hitler-Stalin pact, the Soviet government started drastically shifting its attitude toward the Russian Orthodox and other churches. It mitigated and eventually completely stopped its antireligious campaigns. Many of the "anti-religious museums were either closed down or transformed into church history museums."[37] Stalin met high-ranking bishops; shortly afterward, some of them were appointed to important government and church positions while others were awarded medals for defending the Soviet Union behind the lines. Theological schools began to operate again, and restrictions on religious education for children were relaxed. In return, the Church was expected to endorse the war effort. For example, when Archbishop Sikorski of the Ukrainian Autocephalous Orthodox Church welcomed the German occupation of Ukraine and declared the reestablishment of his church independent from the Russian Orthodox Church, the Russian Orthodox Church excommunicated him.[38] After World War II, the Soviet government continued the same policy, and the Russian Orthodox Church was expected to "consolidate its influence over the Orthodox churches in the Eastern European countries, which were then falling under Soviet control."[39]

The Soviet government's attitude toward the Russian Orthodox Church during and after World War II should not be interpreted as a complete shift away from its antireligious outlook, not to mention from its atheist principles. The antireligious laws, which had not been amended, were interpreted flexibly by the government. In fact, Nikita Khrushchev launched a savage antireligious campaign in 1959 that lasted five years. Two-thirds of the 20,000 then-operating churches were closed down.[40]

The Soviet authorities' antireligious attitude remained fundamentally unchanged throughout the era under their control. Accordingly, the government softened its stance only when it needed to use the Russian Orthodox and other churches' influence for its own political interests. This situation continued until the collapse of the Soviet Union in 1991.

SEPARATION OF CHURCH AND STATE IN THE UNITED STATES

The development of church-state relations in the United States exists in a different context than that in Europe, as there has never been a single dominant "church" or religious institution that competed with the state. America in its early period was a land of immigrants and was composed of numerous colonies and communities with varied religious beliefs. Furthermore, the colonization policy of the United Kingdom prioritized the expansion of the empire through commercial activities and did not necessarily demand the colonies establish the Church of England as their official church. On the side of colonies, too, even though many of them were affiliated with a particular denomination, they needed labor regardless of their religious backgrounds. As a result, the connection between the community and its local church was relatively loose, and the demography was pluralistic across America. Under these circumstances, it was impossible to have a single established church across all the colonies.[41] This was despite the fact that, as John Butler shows, there were some figures who did seek to make the Church of England a single established church for all the colonies, such as James Blair, the then leader of the Church in Virginia.[42]

The early history of church-state relations in the United States is largely characterized by a trend away from state churches, such as the Church of England, and toward more freedom of religion, though many states and communities had been initially associated with some established churches of their European home countries. The trend away from state churches was seen in the establishment of colonies by groups such as the Puritans and Calvinists, who sought to escape religious persecution in England. The trend toward religious freedom was also evident in territories established without an official state church, such as Rhode Island, a community founded by Baptist dissenters.[43]

The Awakening occurred between the early eighteenth and late nineteenth centuries when Americans became less affiliated with established churches and more interested in personal religious experience. The trend was driven by population increase, the influx of immigrants with different religious affiliations, geographical mobility, and the surge of denominationalism.[44] The Awakening led to the development of churches led by lay believers and the growth of grassroots democracy.[45]

The American Revolution was fought in part to secure religious freedom for the people of the United States.[46] This effort was supported by a grassroots movement that included farmers, artisans, homemakers, and other ordinary citizens. The revolution also helped to legitimize independence among the people by making it a religious cause. For example, Thomas Paine's *Common Sense* pamphlet argued that independence was a sacred duty in such statements as: "Even the distance at which the Almighty hath placed England and America, is a strong and natural proof, that the authority of the one, over the other, was never the design of Heaven."[47]

Given the religiously fueled character associated with independence, Americans did not develop an antagonistic attitude toward religion per se. With the presence of pluralistic denominations, the American government deemed it necessary to take a neutral stance toward religions and determined that the best approach was to adopt the separation of church and state.[48] Thomas Jefferson in his letter written in 1802 stated:

> Believing with you that religion is a matter which lies solely between Man & his God, that he owes account to none other for his faith or his worship, that the legitimate powers of government reach actions only, & not opinions, I contemplate with sovereign reverence that act of the whole American people which declared that their legislature should "make no law respecting an establishment of religion, or prohibiting the free exercise thereof," thus building a wall of separation between Church & State.[49]

This idea was incorporated into the First Amendment to the Constitution, guaranteeing the free application of religion and banning the establishment of a state religion. The First Amendment's Establishment Clause not only forbids the government from establishing an official religion but also from taking actions that unduly favor one religion over another. It also prohibits the government from unduly preferring religion over nonreligion and vice versa.[50]

Thus, the separation of church and state in the United States pledges the government's neutrality as it relates to religious denominations. However, it does not mean there are no religious elements in its political sphere, including its president. Robert N. Bellah argues that America is united with a "civil religion." In his essay titled "Civil Religion in America," Bellah contends that the religious dimension of political life in the United States is not only consistent with the separation of church and state principles but also provides core democratic values such as human rights.[51] Bellah cites John F. Kennedy's inaugural address of January 20, 1961: "The rights of man come not from the generosity of the state but from the hand of God." Bellah interprets this statement as stressing the transcendent nature of the "rights of man" that are intact regardless of political structures or situations.[52] Furthermore, emphasizing the religious dimension of the political sphere expressed in Kennedy's address, Bellah writes, "Considering the separation of church and state, how is a president justified in using the word 'God' at all? The answer is that the separation of church and state has not denied the political realm a religious dimension."[53]

The US model of separation of church and state is positively viewed by some scholars such as Saitō Makoto, who states that the United States has been able to develop inclusive values, as opposed to exclusive ones, that connect people who have diverse cultural backgrounds. At the same time, Saitō argues that the future of the United States lies in its continuous endeavors toward preserving this cultural diversity and sharing and achieving the core values guaranteed in the Declaration of Independence that all people are created equal and endowed with unalienable rights to life, liberty, and the pursuit of happiness.[54] Nonetheless, the separation of church and state in the United States has been established on a delicate balance of secular state and religious society. In Alexis de Tocqueville's words, "Religion in America takes no direct part in the government of society, but it must be regarded as the first of their political institutions."[55] Speaking of religious society, statistics show that the vast majority of Americans have religious affiliations: 70 percent of the survey respondents identify themselves as Christians, while 5 percent are affiliated with other religions.[56] Also, 55 percent of the US population prays daily, a percentage that is uniquely high among developed countries.[57] The religious views of the American people can be expressed politically, including through votes for particular legislators or political parties and lobbying through religious institutions. However, the principle of separation of church and state as expressed in the First Amendment forbids preferential treatment of any particular religion and infringement of religious freedom. Thus, the US model of church-state separation remains viable while still allowing the political realm a religious aspect, but only within this limit. Ideally, the religious dimension is expected to contribute to protecting and reinforcing core democratic values such as liberty, equality, and human rights as universal values that are unaffected by earthly political situations.

THE QUASI-THEOCRATIC JUCHE IDEOLOGY IN NORTH KOREA

The Constitution of the Democratic People's Republic of Korea (DPRK) provides for citizens to have the freedom of religious belief. However, it further stipulates that "religion must not be used as a pretext for drawing in foreign forces or for harming the State and social order," thereby in practice limiting the exercise of the right to freedom of religion.[58] Historically, after the Korean War (1950–1953), former Leader Kim Il Sung viewed religion as the "opiate of the people," claiming it was used as a tool for imperialism.[59] Today, many official documents report continuous, serious violations of human rights, including the freedom of religion, in the DPRK. According to a UN report, the government of the DPRK is "engaged in a systematic and widespread attack against people considered a threat to the country's political system, including people who practice religion."[60] The US government's 2021 Report on International Religious Freedom states that the DPRK authorities continue to "execute, torture, arrest, and physically abuse individuals engaged in almost any religious activities."[61] A North

Korean defector's testimonial cited in a South Korean government-funded think tank's 2019 white paper says, "North Korea oppresses religion . . . because of the sense that the one-person dictatorship can be undermined by religious faith."[62] According to the 2020 version of the white paper, while DPRK continues its religious persecution, it uses what appear to be religious facilities such as churches and temples only for "political purposes and external propaganda" for visitors from abroad.[63] For example, when foreign guests visited a church in Pyongyang, government officials carefully selected and gathered several hundred citizens to participate in "fake church services."[64] Firmly maintaining its antireligious stance, DPRK "does not allow any ideology other than its official *Juche* ideology, which is the official ideology of the state."[65] Other religions or ideologies are not tolerated because they would be "regarded as a serious threat" to DPRK's state system.[66]

Many English texts translate Juche as "self-reliance."[67] However, its concept flummoxes outsiders partly because the state authorities have discretionally changed the doctrine's meaning over time "depending on the needs of the North Korean leadership."[68] In other words, Juche has basically meant "whatever the North Korean government needed it to mean."[69] In fact, the survival of the DPRK's repressive regime is in no small part attributable to Juche being used to successfully convince the country's people of the legitimacy of its government.[70]

Most strikingly, as many scholars argue, the Juche philosophy and reverence for the Kim family resemble a form of "state-sponsored theology."[71] Though Juche has been consistently defined by the state authorities as a "revolutionary new atheistic philosophy," it has been increasingly given "profound religious implications."[72] In fact, as Shin argues, the religious dimension of Juche is a major factor that has helped DPRK "maintain its own political system at such a level of intensity" and Kim Il Sung's "cultic system" for nearly half a century.[73] Originally, Kim Il Sung developed the principles of Juche shortly after the end of the Korean War (1950–1953). His then unstable power base prompted him to deploy ideological purges in order to solidify his political position, using the Juche principles of national solidarity "as a domestic instrument of personal cult-building."[74] Despite the DPRK's emphasis on Juche's consistency with Marxism-Leninism, Juche as a philosophical thought shows discrepancy from Marist-Leninist principles, especially in that Juche upholds the necessity of an "exceptionally brilliant and outstanding leader" in the mobilization of the masses of the working class.[75] Kim Il Sung's regime used an analogy drawn from human anatomy to stress the importance of the "Great Leader" being the brain that makes decisions and issues orders through the nerve system, the party, to the bone and muscle, the people.[76] Juche thereby helped establish Kim Il Sung's "god-like status."[77] It has thus "developed into the elaborate indigenous national religion of North Korea."[78]

The idolization of Kim Il Sung has been further reinforced since the declaration of the Ten Principles of Unitary Ideology in 1974, which mandates that every North Korean owes "unconditional loyalty to Kim Il Sung and follow[s] Kim Il Sung's instructions as absolute guidance."[79] These principles sought to "deify 'the Great Leader' Kim Il Sung, and have spiritually commanded the behaviors of North Koreans more than any other laws and regulations."[80] Kim Jong Un, the grandson of Kim Il Sung and the DPRK's state head since 2012, revised the Ten Principles in 2013, changing its name to the Ten Principles to Firmly Establish the Party's Unitary Leadership system. Having superiority over the Constitution, the revised Ten Principles "governs the standards that systematically safeguard Kim Jong Un's unitary dictatorship."[81] The revised Ten Principles are used arbitrarily by the DPRK's authorities to penalize citizens whom they consider "political or ideological criminals" for any reason.[82] For example, the state authorities used the Ten Principles to make a family "disappear" after their nine-year-old child scribbled on the faces of Kim Il Sung and Kim Jong Il in his/her school textbook.[83]

Elevated to the level of religion as the sole source of legitimacy, Juche has served as an effective tool for the DPRK authorities to use to exploit their people, including when implementing their economic and defense policies. For example, in food and other production activities, Juche becomes "another element of control" as it demands "self-reliance," in practice requiring that people increase production through "more enthusiastic labour and longer hours."[84] Juche's emphasis on self-reliant defense capability led to the development of the Military First (Songun) doctrine, an addendum to Juche, when DPRK in the 1990s faced a devastating famine after losing its primary source of food aid from the Soviet Union due to its fall. Songun was used as justification for feeding soldiers before ordinary citizens to avoid "risking a military coup."[85] Songun also served to justify the state's development and deployment of nuclear weapons despite international sanctions that have further hurt the country's economy.[86] As of 2020, DPRK's military spending accounted for around 24 percent of its gross domestic product (GDP), making North Korea first in the world in terms of military spending as a percentage of GDP.[87] These policies have been enforced despite the fact that 60 percent of the people are estimated to live below the poverty line.[88] The implementation of these apparently unreasonable policies has been legitimized with the Juche belief system whose interpretations have been "tailored to fit the needs of the North Korean government at the time."[89]

Juche's religious dimension has been effectively used to help the Kim family and its entourage maintain their hold on power for such a long period. In short, Juche amounts to a quasi-theocracy that is used by the DPRK's state authorities to manipulate its people. Dennis P. Halpin finds "surprising parallels" between DPRK's Juche and Japan's State Shinto, the cult of the emperor that existed until the end of World War II, which will be elaborated on in chapters 3 and 4 of this book, in multiple ways.[90] These two ideologies, both created by their respective states, resemble each other in many aspects, including the denial of any other ideology or religion, restrictions on the right to freedom of religion, and their theocratical nature.

THE CONSTITUTIONAL PROTECTION OF RELIGIONS FREEDOM CONTRASTED WITH ACTUAL CASES OF RELIGIOUS VIOLENCE AND UNDUE RELIGIOUS INFLUENCE ON THE STATE—THE CONFLICTS BETWEEN MUSLIM, HINDU, AND GOVERNMENT INSTITUTIONS IN CONTEMPORARY INDIA

India is a multicultural, multiethnic, multilinguistic, and multireligious country. Hindus comprise a dominant majority, approximately 80 percent of India's population; 94 percent of the world's Hindus live in India. Muslims also account for a significant population, approximately 15 percent; India is home to one of the world's largest Muslim populations.[91] With the aim of avoiding religious conflicts, India's Constitution prohibits discrimination on the grounds of religion, among other attributes, and guarantees religious freedom. The word "secular" is explicitly included in its preamble. These characteristics of the Constitution reflect the ideas of leaders who fought for India's independence, including some who suffered fatal reactionary responses. Mahatma Gandhi, who was himself a Hindu who advocated a secular state free from discrimination, was assassinated in 1948 by a Hindu nationalist. Jawaharlal Nehru, the country's first prime minister, asserted that secularism was imperative for building a peaceful society. Since India's independence, however, Muslims have constantly faced "systemic discrimination, prejudice, and violence despite constitutional protections."[92] This is because, despite Nehru's policy being implemented with the best of intentions, successors used this legacy to "gain political mileage and used minorities as vote banks by constantly keeping alive their fears of a majority domination."[93]

It is, nevertheless, more recently that anti-Muslim sentiments have sharply risen, with violence increasing alarmingly. Underlying this violence is Hindutva ideology, a political ideology that views India as a Hindu nation and defines Indian culture in terms of Hindu cultural values. Among its core beliefs is its justification of the use of violence for achieving its goal of establishing a Hindu state. At the forefront of such violence is the Sangh Parivar, a conglomerate of Hindu nationalist organizations including the Bharatiya Janata Party (BJP) with the aim of making secular India a Hindu state. It has been gaining momentum, especially since 2014 when BJP won a ruling majority in the general election and the Narendra Modi administration came into power.[94] BJP has since pursued a Hindu nationalist agenda. In 2019, the BJP-led parliament passed and Modi signed the Citizenship Amendment Act, which allows immigrants coming to India from Pakistan, Afghanistan, and Bangladesh to obtain citizenship promptly if they are Hindu, Sikh, Buddhist, Jain, Parsi, or Christian, but excluding Pakistani Muslims. Protests broke out across the country after this development, but these also became the target of a violent crackdown by the police, with over fifty people dead. Furthermore, Modi has eliminated the special political autonomy of Muslim-majority Kashmir by way of revocation of Article 370 of the Constitution, allowing, among other things, people from outside Kashmir to purchase real estate properties and settle in Kashmir. This move is seen by many as aiming to change the demographic character of the region and undermine the Muslim majority there. Moreover, this was followed by a violent crackdown on the insurgency movement against the Indian government within the region.[95] On April 10, 2022, a day of celebration marking the Hindu god Ram's birthday, major clashes between Hindus and Muslims occurred in six states. Videos posted on social media showed scenes of crowds of men, "many waving weapons, whipped into a fervor by chants hailing Lord Ram."[96]

The recent situation in India is an obvious departure from the principles of the secular state and religious freedom embedded in the country's Constitution. The core secular values promoted in the early days of the Republic of India have deteriorated with the rise of religious nationalism. This negative religious influence on the state exists despite the constitutional guarantee of equality and religious freedom. This indicates that religious freedom, a core value of democracy, is not respected as a universal value that should not be affected by political power structures or neutralized by particular religious denominations.

CONCLUSION

The paradigms shown in this chapter have broadly discussed the situations of the state and religion relationships in several Western and non-Western countries. The section on Western Europe briefly reviewed the history of the church and state relations in the region, leading to secularization. This chapter then discussed the country-specific cases of the United Kingdom, a constitutional monarchy; Russia, with a focus on the conflict and compromise between Orthodox Christianity and the atheist USSR; the separation of church and state in the United States; the quasi-theocratic ideology of North Korea; and the conflicts between Muslim and Hindu practitioners and religious influence on the state in India.

These country-specific cases are by no means exhaustive in terms of scope. They nonetheless illustrate the complexity and tensions that are consistently observed with respect to the relations between the state and religions or religious institutions. No case indicates the end of the matter; every case calls for continuous monitoring and analysis.

NOTES

1. Dennis C. Mueller, "The State and Religion," *Review of Social Economy* 71, no. 1 (2013): 1–19, https://doi.org/10.1080/00346764.2012.681115 (May 15, 2023).

2. Mueller, "State and Religion," 2–4.

3. Mueller, "State and Religion," 2–4.

4. Carl A. Volz, *The Medieval Church: From the Dawn of the Middle Ages to the Eve of the Reformation* (Nashville: Abingdon Press, 2011).

5. Volz, *Medieval Church*, 17–22.

6. Volz, *Medieval Church*, 17–22.

7. George Holmes, *The Oxford History of Medieval Europe* (Oxford and New York: Oxford University Press, 2001).

8. Holmes, *Oxford History*, 145–65.

9. Holmes, *Oxford History*, 165–72.

10. Holmes, *Oxford History*, 165–72.

11. Volz, *Medieval Church*, 62–89.

12. Holmes, *Oxford History*, 276–90.

13. Henry Kamen, *Early Modern European Society* (New York: Routledge, 2000), 38–58.

14. Richard Falk, *Religion and Humane Global Governance* (New York: Palgrave, 2001), 39.

15. James Holt, "John: King of England," *Encyclopedia Britannica*, https://www.britannica.com/biography/John-king-of-England/Quarrel-with-the-church (May 5, 2023).

16. Charlotte Methuen, "The English Reformation in Wittenberg: Luther and Melanchthon's Engagement with Religious Change in England 1521–1560," *Reformation & Renaissance Review* 20, no. 3 (2018): 8–9.

17. BBC, "Christianity in Britain," https://www.bbc.co.uk/religion/religions/christianity/history/uk_1.shtml (May 5, 2023).

18. BBC, "Christianity in Britain."

19. John Black, *Reign of Elizabeth (1558–1603)* (Oxford: Clarendon Press, 1949), 13–15.

20. Rebecca Catto, Grace Davie, and David Perfect, "State and Religion in Great Britain: Constitutional Foundations, Religious Minorities, the Law and Education," *Insight Turkey* 17, no. 1 (Winter 2015): 81.

21. David Torrance, *The Relationship Between Church and State in the United Kingdom* (London: House of Commons Library, 2021), 6.

22. John Curtice, Elizabeth Clery, Jane Perry, Miranda Phillips, and Nilufer Rahim, eds., *British Social Attitudes: The 36th Report* (London: The National Centre for Social Research, 2019), 22, https://www.bsa.natcen.ac.uk/ (May 5, 2023).

23. Michael Holden, "Young British People Want to Ditch the Monarchy, Poll Suggests," *Reuters*, May 21, 2021, https://www.reuters.com/world/uk/young-british-people-want-ditch-monarchy-poll-suggests-2021-05-20/ (May 5, 2023).

24. David Bebbington, "Religion and National Feeling in Nineteenth-Century Wales and Scotland," in *Religion and National Identity*, ed. Stuart Mews (Oxford: Basil Blackwell, 1982), 501.

25. Aizawa Hisashi, *Gendai kokka ni okeru shūkyō to seiji* [Religion and politics in the contemporary states] (Tokyo: Keiso Shobo, 1966), 302.

26. This does not mean that the church-state relationship was consistently stable. There had been competitive periods as well as periods of certain levels of revival of other religious denominations.

27. Francis Fukuyama, "The Modernizing Imperative: The USSR as an Ordinary Country," *National Interest*, no. 31 (1993): 16, http://www.jstor.org/stable/42894852.

28. Paul Froese, "Forced Secularization in Soviet Russia: Why an Atheistic Monopoly Failed," *Journal for the Scientific Study of Religion* 43, no. 1 (2004): 35, http://www.jstor.org/stable/1387772.

29. David Kowalewski, "Protest for Religious Rights in the USSR: Characteristics and Consequences," *Russian Review* 39, no. 4 (October 1980): 426, https://www.jstor.org/stable/128810 (May 15, 2023).

30. Kowalewski, "Protest for Religious Rights," 426.

31. Philip Walters, "The Russian Orthodox Church and the Soviet State," *The Annals of the American Academy of Political and Social Science* 483 (1986): 136–37, http://www.jstor.org/stable/1045546 (May 5, 2023).

32. Falk, *Religion*, 43.

33. Committee on Foreign Affairs, House of Representatives, *Religious Persecution in the Soviet Union (Part II): Hearing before the Subcommittee on Europe and the Middle East and on Human Rights and International Organizations of the Committee on Foreign Affairs, House of Representatives; Ninety-Ninth Congress, Second Session, 30 July 1986* (Washington, DC: US Government Printing Office, 1986), 6.

34. Aizawa, *Gendai kokka* [Contemporary states], 309.

35. Walters, "Russian Orthodox Church," 138.

36. Walters, "Russian Orthodox Church," 139.

37. Aizawa, *Gendai kokka* [Contemporary states], 310.

38. Aizawa, *Gendai kokka* [Contemporary states], 310–11.

39. Walters, "Russian Orthodox Church," 139.

40. Walters, "Russian Orthodox Church," 142.

41. Saitō Makoto, "Amerika kakumei to shūkyō" [American Revolution and religion], in *Amerika to shūkyō* [America and religion], ed. Mori Kōichi (Tokyo: Japan Institute of International Affairs, 1997), 71.

42. John Butler, "Coercion, Miracle, Reason: Rethinking the American Religious Experience in the Revolutionary Age," in *Religion in a Revolutionary Age*, ed. Ronald Hoffman and Peter J. Albert (Charlottesville: The University Press of Virginia, 1994), 5.

43. John Wilson and Donald Drakeman, *Church and State in American History: Key Documents, Decisions, and Commentary from Five Centuries* (Oxfordshire: Routledge, 2019), 34.

44. Saitō, "Amerika kakumei" [American Revolution], 71–72.

45. Saitō, "Amerika kakumei" [American Revolution], 77.

46. John Wilson, "Religion and Revolution in American History," *The Journal of Interdisciplinary History* 23, no. 3 (1993): 606, https://doi.org/10.2307/206104 (May 15, 2023).

47. Thomas Paine, *Common Sense*, Pamphlet, 1776, https://oll.libertyfund.org/page/1776-paine-common-sense-pamphlet.

48. Aizawa, *Gendai kokka* [Contemporary states], 199–207.

49. Thomas Jefferson, "Jefferson's Letter to the Danbury Baptists," 1802, https://www.loc.gov/loc/lcib/9806/danpre.html (May 5, 2023).

50. Cornell Law School, "Establishment Clause," https://www.law.cornell.edu/wex/establishment_clause (September 22, 2022).

51. Robert N. Bellah, "Civil Religion in America," *Daedalus* 96, no. 1 (1967): 1–21, https://www.jstor.org/stable/20027022 (May 5, 2023).

52. Bellah, "Civil Religion in America," 4.

53. Bellah, "Civil Religion in America," 3.

54. Saitō, "Amerika kakumei" [American Revolution], 88.

55. Alexis de Tocqueville, *Democracy in America*, vol. 1, trans. Henry Reeve, electric ed. (Charlottesville: University of Virginia, 1997), https://xroads.virginia.edu/~Hyper/DETOC/1_ch17.htm (May 15, 2023).

56. PRRI Staff, "The American Religious Landscape in 2020," *PRRI*, July 8, 2021, https://www.prri.org/research/2020-census-of-american-religion/ (May 5, 2023).

57. Jeff Diamant, "With High Level of Prayer, US Is an Outlier Among Wealthy Nations," *Pew Research Center*, May 1, 2019, https://www.pewresearch.org/fact-tank/2019/05/01/with-high-levels-of-prayer-u-s-is-an-outlier-among-wealthy-nations/ (May 5, 2023).

58. United Nations General Assembly, *Report of the Special Rapporteur to the 76th session of the General Assembly: On the Situation of Human Rights in the Democratic People's Republic of Korea*, A/76/392, October 8, 2021: 9–10, https://www.ohchr.org/en/documents/country-reports/a76392-report-special-rapporteur-76th-session-general-assembly (May 5, 2023).

59. UN General Assembly, *Situation of Human Rights*, 10.

60. United Nations Humans Rights Council, *Promoting Accountability in the Democratic People's Republic of Korea: Report of the United Nations High*

Commissioner for Human Rights, A/HR/46/52, January 11, 2021: 9, https://digitallibrary.un.org/record/3898922 (May 5, 2023).

61. US Department of State, *2021 Report on International Religious Freedom: Democratic People's Republic of Korea (DPRK)*, Office of International Religious Freedom, June 2, 2021, https://www.state.gov/reports/2021-report-on-international-religious-freedom/north-korea/ (May 5, 2023).

62. Sookyung Kim, Kyu-chang Lee, Kyung-ok Do, and Jea-hwan Hong, *White Paper on Human Rights in North Korea 2019* (Seoul: Korean Institute for National Unification, 2019), 187, https://www.kinu.or.kr/main/eng (May 5, 2023).

63. Kyu-chang Lee, Sookyung Kim, Ji Sun Yee, Eun Mee Jeong, and Yejoon Rim, *White Paper on Human Rights in North Korea 2020* (Seoul: Korean Institute for National Unification, 2020), 203.

64. Lee et al., *North Korea 2020*, 203.

65. Gyeong-seob Oh, Hong Suk-hoon, Hong Jea-hwan, Jeong Eun-mee, and Yee Ji-sun, *White Paper on Human Rights in North Korea 2021* (Seoul: Korea Institute for National Unification, 2021), 215.

66. Oh et al., *North Korea 2021*, 215.

67. Geir Helgesen, "Political Revolution in a Cultural Continuum: Preliminary Observations on the North Korean 'Juche' Ideology," *Asian Perspective* 15, no. 1 (1991): 189, http://www.jstor.org/stable/42705297 (May 15, 2023).

68. Zack Beauchamp, "Juche, the State Ideology That Makes North Koreans Revere Kim Jong Un, Explained," *Vox*, June 18, 2018, https://www.vox.com/world/2018/6/18/17441296/north-korea-propaganda-ideology-juche (May 5, 2023).

69. Beauchamp, "Juche."

70. Beauchamp, "Juche."

71. US Department of State, *2021 Report: Democratic People's Republic of Korea.*

72. Eun Hee Shin, "The Sociopolitical Organism: The Religious Dimensions of Juche Philosophy," in Religions of Korea in Practice, ed. Robert E. Buswell (Princeton: Princeton University Press, 2018), 519.

73. Shin, "Sociopolitical Organism," 522.

74. Grace Lee, "The Political Philosophy of Juche," *Stanford Journal of East Asian Affairs* 3, no. 1 (Spring 2003): 108.

75. Lee, "Political Philosophy," 111.

76. Lee, "Political Philosophy," 111.

77. Lee, "Political Philosophy," 111.

78. Shin, "Sociopolitical Organism," 517.

79. Oh et al., *North Korea 2021*, 216.

80. Oh et al., *North Korea 2021*, 216.

81. Oh et al., *North Korea 2021*, 216.

82. Oh et al., *North Korea 2021*, 218.

83. Oh et al., *North Korea 2021*, 218.

84. United Nations Human Rights Council, *Report of the Detailed Findings of the Commission of Inquiry on Human Rights in the Democratic People's Republic of Korea*, A/HR/25/CRP, February 7, 2014, 3, https://www.ohchr.org/en/hr-bodies/hrc/co-idprk/reportofthe-commissionof-inquiry-dprk (May 5, 2023).

85. Beauchamp, "Juche."

86. Beauchamp, "Juche."

87. US Department of State, *World Military Expenditures and Arms Transfers 2021*, December 31, 2021, https://www.state.gov/world-military-expenditures-and-arms-transfers-2021-edition/ (May 5, 2023).

88. Jesus Crespo Cuaresma, Olha Danylo, Steffen Fritz, Martin Hofer, Homi Kharas, and Juan Carlos, "What Do We Know About Poverty in North Korea?" Palgrave Communications 6, no. 40 (2020): 2–3, https://doi.org/10.1057/s41599-020-0417-4 (May 15, 2023).

89. Beauchamp, "Juche."

90. Dennis P. Halpin, "North Korea's Kim Family Cult: Roots in Japanese State Shinto?" *NK News*, February 19, 2015, https://www.nknews.org/2015/02/north-koreas-kim-family-cult-roots-in-state-shinto/ (May 5, 2023).

91. Stephanie Kramer, "Religious Composition of India," Pew Research Center, September 21, 2021, https://www.pewresearch.org/religion/2021/09/21/religious-composition-of-india/ (May 5, 2023).

92. Lindsay Maizland, "India's Muslims: An Increasingly Marginalized Population," Council on Foreign Relations, https://www.cfr.org/backgrounder/india-muslims-marginalized-population-bjp-modi (May 5, 2023).

93. Amadendu Misra, "Hindu Nationalism and Muslim Minority Rights in India," *International Journal on Minority and Group Rights* 7, no. 1 (2000): 3, http://www.jstor.org/stable/24675146 (May 15, 2023).

94. Sudha Ramachandran, "Hindutva Violence in India: Trends and Implications," *Counter Terrorist Trends and Analyses* 12, no. 4 (2020): 15–16, https://www.jstor.org/stable/26918077.

95. Eman Atta Maan, "The Hindu-Muslim Conflict Under Modi," *Traileoni*, March 26, 2021, https://traileoni.it/2021/05/the-hindu-muslim-conflict-under-modi (May 5, 2023).

96. Gerry Shin and Anant Gupta, "Religious Clashes Across India Spark Fears of Further Violence," *Washington Post*, April 20, 2022, https://www.washingtonpost.com/world/2022/04/20/india-hindu-muslim-communal-violence (May 5, 2023).

Chapter 2

Religion's Place in Domestic and Foreign Policy

Case Studies from the Twentieth to Twenty-First Centuries

This chapter provides case studies on the influences of religious institutions on foreign policies and domestic politics of some major countries. The first three sections focus on the United States. The first section reviews former president Jimmy Carter's emphasis on human rights in foreign policy and its connection to his religious convictions. The second section analyzes former president George W. Bush's use of religion in justifying his decision to conduct a military attack on Iraq. The third section discusses the disproportionate influence of the religious right on US domestic politics, including the recent issue of abortion. The fourth section considers Russia's war with Ukraine in terms of the relevance of religion. The last section elaborates on the case of Japan in contrast to the West in terms of the history of the state and its religious relationships. Thus, this chapter adds context to the Japan-specific discussions being made in the following chapters.

FORMER US PRESIDENT JIMMY CARTER'S FOCUS ON HUMAN RIGHTS IN FOREIGN POLICY

From the first day of his term of office, former US President Jimmy Carter set out to fundamentally alter the direction of American foreign policy by shaping it around the principles of human rights, marking a break with traditional Cold War diplomacy where the "effort to contain communism dominated American policy and overrode all other concerns."[1] Carter's emphasis on human rights as the centerpiece of his administration's foreign policy, as many point out, stemmed largely from his religious conviction. William Steding, for example, demonstrates based on an extensive analysis of Carter's writings and statements that the former president's "selection of human rights as his thematic approach to foreign policy was strongly supported by his religious permissions, standards, and convictions."[2]

Carter's human-rights foreign policies, as Friedbert Pflüger puts it, "emerged as the antithesis to Henry Kissinger's realpolitik."[3] The former president believed that continued support for other countries' dictatorships despite their infringement of human rights for the sake of deterring the rise of communism was "not merely against American ideals but harmed the nation's self-interest."[4] Although many commentators criticized Carter's policy as simplistic and naive, the close examination by David F. Schmitz and Vanessa Walker of the Carter administration's development of its foreign policy demonstrates that this critique is "wrong on both counts" and that the administration's commitment to advocating human rights was not "rhetorical or naïve."[5] Even Carter's national security advisor Zbigniew Brzezinski, who consistently advised in favor of a tough line against the Soviet Union, also supported Carter's foreign policy based on human rights, a shift from the traditional policy dictated by US-Soviet relations. Brzezinski endorses Carter's policy prioritizing human rights, stating that the call to overcome the nation's "inordinate fear of Communism" was not "a dismissal of the reality of Soviet power."[6] Moreover, Brzezinski "felt strongly that a major emphasis on human rights as a component of U.S. foreign policy would advance America's global interests" by demonstrating the "reality of our democratic system, in sharp contrast to the political system and practices of our adversaries."[7] Throughout his time in office, Carter consistently maintained his commitment to the advocacy of human rights even in the face of a series of crises for the administration. These included Moscow sending its troops into Afghanistan, causing a shift in the US stance toward the Soviet Union from détente to confrontation and the US-friendly dictator Anastasio Somoza being overthrown by the communist Sandinistas in Nicaragua.[8] Schmitz and Walker describe the dilemma the Carter administration faced in the crisis of Nicaragua: "Carter had to defend his actions against charges that he was abandoning an ally and opening the door to communism in Central America while simultaneously being criticized for supporting a flagrant perpetrator of human rights violations."[9] After trying unsuccessfully to persuade Somoza to reform his government and respect human rights, the Carter administration concluded that the only solution was to cease its support for Somoza. It is worth noting that the "administration did not support Somoza and instead upheld its policy of human rights and non-intervention. Unlike previous administrations, it did not see only two alternatives, the dictator or communism."[10] Consistency in this policy was maintained throughout the world, though through different approaches based on realistic political analysis of each country's situation. In Brzezinski's words, "Though it was difficult for all of us to find the proper balance between human-rights imperatives and the uglier realities of world politics, our human-rights policy did mean freedom for many individuals around the world."[11] In fact, the human rights policy implemented by the administration had a quantifiable impact, including the Indonesian government releasing fifteen thousand political prisoners over a period of eight months in 1977–1978 and completing the release of the remaining twenty thousand over the next two years.[12] Carter's foreign policy based on human rights was thus neither naive nor rhetorical.

Naturally, however, this does not mean Carter's foreign policy was flawless. One example of a major setback is the case of Iran, where Carter was unable to effectively address the human rights issues stemming from the Shah's regime. Misguided by political intelligence provided by the Central Intelligence Agency and US diplomatic delegates in Tehran, the Carter administration continued to support the Shah despite his continued human rights violations until the Iranian Revolution overthrew his regime in 1979, which contributed disastrously to Carter's political defeat. According to Brzezinski, better quality intelligence could have enabled the Carter administration to pursue a better course of action in Iran.[13] This failure demonstrates the difficulties and complexities involved in the implementation of Carter's foreign policy prioritizing human rights, especially in such a case as Iran where there was a mutual reliance. While Iran relied on US financial and military assistance, the Carter administration needed stability and could not afford political turmoil in its ally which might put at risk the American and Western interests in the oil region of the Persian Gulf and make it vulnerable to Soviet Union intrusion.[14] That being said, unsatisfactory outcomes do not in themselves negate the overall consistency of Carter's human rights policy. Ironically and against the administration's intention, Carter's pressure on the Shah to improve the human rights situation, while it met with very limited success, contributed to fueling the uprising of the oppressed Iranian people which eventually caused the fall of the Shah.[15]

Though with varying outcomes, Carter's foreign policy decisions upheld his emphasis on human rights, a focus for which his religious convictions significantly accounted. It is of interest to note that Brzezinski also acknowledges that the Carter administration's "commitment to human rights reflected the former president's own religious beliefs, as well as his political acumen."[16] The then national security advisor adds, Carter "deeply believed in human rights and that commitment remained constant during his Administration."[17]

These assessments of the Carter administration's emphasis on human rights as reflecting the former president's religious faith are affirmed by Carter's own account:

> Unlike other living creatures, humans are capable of self-reflection, worship, and of morality; . . . humans will have to evolve and implement fair and equitable treatment among ourselves, which could come close to the Universal Declaration of Human Rights. . . . Our personal responsibility is to strive to do better, perhaps to reach for moral and ethical goals that at times seem to be out of reach. This is the realm of religion, so this means we must be free of restraint by others in order to be such innovative activists.[18]

In his presidential inauguration address, Carter stated, "Our commitment to human rights must be absolute."[19] "There is no way to understand me and my political philosophy," he said on another occasion, "without understanding my faith."[20] At the same time, while being a devoted Christian, Carter rejected fundamentalism and intolerance toward other denominations or religions. He writes, "The aim of most religions has been to preserve our highest ideals, apply them to current circumstances, and of course extend them to as many people as possible."[21] He specifically criticizes and expresses his concern about fundamentalism, writing, "The Christians who resist the inclination toward fundamentalism and who follow the nature, actions, and words of Jesus Christ should consider people who are different from us to be worthy of our care, generosity, forgiveness, compassion, and unselfish love."[22]

Carter's rejection of the inclination toward religious fundamentalism or conservatism with a discriminatory interpretation of theology and his adherence to a more universal interpretation are also reflected in the denominations that he chose to be associated with. As Stephen Rock says, though Carter was by affiliation a member of the Southern Baptist Convention (SBC), which is now a largely evangelical denomination, it is important to note that in his formative years as well as during the years of his presidency the SBC was considerably less conservative than it is today. It was not until the 1990s that "a fundamentalist movement . . . managed to take control of the SBC's seminaries and drive moderate Baptists from leadership positions in the seminaries and the Convention itself."[23] In fact, Carter "dissociated himself from the SBC in 2000."[24] Rock's analysis aligns with Carter's own statement that his religious beliefs were "shared with the Southern Baptist Convention (SBC) until a more conservative group acquired practical control of the convention and adopted some guiding principles with which [he] did not agree."[25] Referring to SBC's rules against women, Carter says, "This contradicts my interpretation of the life and teachings of Jesus, which exemplified equal status of all people."[26] Carter maintained this view during his presidency as well as after leaving the White House. He says that he was "relieved when more moderate (or traditional) Baptists formed the Cooperative Baptist Fellowship (CBF)."[27] The international organization of Carter's present denomination is "the Baptist World Alliance, formed in 1905 and including about 48 million members, which the CBF has joined and from which SBC has resigned."[28]

In 1977, Carter signed the International Covenant on Civil and Political Rights and the International Covenant on Economic, Social, and Cultural Rights, which had not been signed by his predecessors for more than a decade. As Pflüger argues, scarcely does a multinational conference take place today without touching on the issue of human rights, whether at the United Nations or the Conference for Security and Cooperation in Europe. Hardly a credit is granted, or foreign aid approved, without previous inspection of an administration's human rights situation. Since the middle of the 1970s, the principles of human rights have steadily gained in importance.[29] As Pflüger adds,

> To attribute this to a single person or a particular policy would be an exaggeration. But it was President Jimmy Carter, from the moment of his oath of office on January 20th, 1977, who began to use that office to propagate the idea of human rights throughout the world. The unleashing of human rights as a topic on the agenda of international politics will thus remain bound to the name of Jimmy Carter.[30]

Carter's efforts to develop a post-Cold War foreign policy based on human rights dramatically changed the discourse on American foreign policy and made it a central concern of American diplomacy. The idea of human rights is, as Schmitz and Walker conclude in their article, "now a fixture on the policy agenda and part of both American and world discussions of international relations. . . . It provided support to those abroad struggling against abusive and dictatorial governments, led to the release of political prisoners . . . , and forced governments to modify their behavior or risk losing American support and aid."[31] This change is the most significant of the efforts Carter made to "forge a post-Cold War foreign policy for the United States that rejected the world view of the containment doctrine and sought to introduce American ideals into the making of the nation's foreign policy."[32] For Carter, such ideals, including the advocacy of human rights, were infused with his religious beliefs. The religious elements in the political sphere are accepted within the American model of the separation of church and state, as we have discussed in chapter 1, because they are ideally expected to reinforce such democratic and universal values as human rights. Carter's foreign policy centered on human rights presents an example endeavoring to fulfill such an expectation.

RELIGIOUS JUSTIFICATION BY FORMER PRESIDENT GEORGE W. BUSH FOR THE INVASION OF IRAQ

The presidents of the United States, since its earliest days, have never eschewed from the religious dimensions of their political discourse, including in their public addresses. Furthermore, in their rhetoric, they even "emphasize religious symbols and transcendent principles to engender a sense of unity and shared national identity."[33] This is generally viewed favorably by the US public.[34] The religious dimension of the political sphere in the United States is accepted based on the expectation that it serves to strengthen the transcendent nature of core democratic values such as liberty and human rights, in that they are not affected by the earthly political situation. Nonetheless, this concept does not alter the principle of separation of church and state that requires the state and its institutions, including the presidency, to be neutral to all religions and religious denominations and to prevent their policies from undue influence or favoritism. In the case of George W. Bush, however, his own religious convictions were heavily reflected in government policies, notably in his decision to attack Iraq after 9/11. As Jim Wallis analyzes, Bush believed that those who were not with America were on the wrong side of the "divine confrontation."[35] His religiously motivated military action received public disapproval, including from mainstream Christian churches, creating a complex case of tensions between church and state represented by the presidency. Bush, in his decision to begin the Iraq War, is considered by scholars including David Dumke to have demonstrated political and religious fundamentalism.[36] Dumke makes this assertion based on his research of hundreds of Bush administration public communications, finding four characteristics rooted in religious fundamentalism supporting its political decisions and actions: simplistic conceptions of the political landscape, notably good versus evil; calls for immediate action as a necessary part of the nation's calling; declarations about the will of God for America; and claims that dissent from the administration is unpatriotic.[37] In fact, the overt influence of Bush's religious conviction on his foreign policy was revealed in his claim that "he was on a mission from God when he launched the invasions of Afghanistan and Iraq."[38] When Bush met diplomatic delegates from Palestine and Israel during their summit in Egypt four months after the US-led invasion of Iraq in 2003, he told them, "I am driven with a mission from God. God would tell me, 'George, go get and fight these terrorists in Afghanistan.' And I did. And then God would tell me 'George, go and end the tyranny in Iraq.' And I did."[39]

Bush's interpretation of God's will, however, was not endorsed by mainstream Christian churches. Many of them issued statements against Bush's attack on Iraq, including American Baptist Churches, the Christian Church (Disciples of Christ), and the Evangelical Lutheran Church in America.[40] It was rejected even by his own Methodist church. Prior to the Bush administration's military attacks on Iraq, Jim Winker, head of United Methodism's General Board of Church and Society, the international public policy and social justice agency of the Church, was quoted as saying the president's intended war was "without any justification according to the teaching of Christ," adding that "all attempts at a 'dialogue' between the President and his own church over the war had fallen on deaf ears at the White House."[41] In his official statement, Winker stresses the fact that Bush's intended war is condemned by his own church: "United Methodists have a particular duty to speak out against an unprovoked attack. President Bush and Vice-President Cheney are members of our denomination."[42] Furthermore, urging Bush to respect international laws, Winker rejected the self-defense justification of the Bush administration's military attacks, saying, "No case can be made that a war against Iraq is justified for the self-defense of the United States."[43]

The Bush administration's invasion of Iraq, in fact, exceeded the scope of self-defense accepted by international laws, including the UN Charter. This is the case even when allowing for a stretched interpretation of the right of self-defense, where the use of force might be allowed as it is not reasonable to expect a country to risk its security if confronted with an immediate threat.[44] In particular, it was problematic that the Bush administration initiated "a major war without any pretense of responding in the spirit of self-defense."[45] As Falk states, Bush's attack on Iraq thus "seems so clearly to qualify as a war of aggression."[46] It is ironic that "in combating the Islamic extremists responsible for Sept. 11, the administration has crafted, pursued, and engendered its own brand of political fundamentalism—one that . . . functions ideologically in a manner similar to the version offered by the terrorists."[47]

Given the very strong authority given to the president of the United States, a country that many have considered an example of democracy, his/her decisions and actions are expected to be guided by the rule of law, not by religious conviction. However, as Brigitte P. Volochinsky argues, Bush "gave into temptation when he acted religiously on his own, possibly fallible, interpretations of world events."[48] Actions guided by the rule of law are consistent with the separation of church and state, in that religious beliefs are denied inappropriate influence on the decisions of the political sphere. Religious considerations are valid and ideally would support the transcendental nature of core democratic values. However, in this case, the religiously inflected discourse of the

US presidency eroded that religious neutrality and thus amounted to a violation of the separation of church and state principle established in the First Amendment.

THE OUTSIZE INFLUENCE OF THE RELIGIOUS RIGHT ON DOMESTIC POLITICS AND GOVERNMENT POLICY IN THE UNITED STATES

The First Amendment to the US Constitution, under the Establishment and Free Exercise clauses, protects diversity in religious views while ensuring the government remains neutral in relation to matters of faith. However, when Texas governor Greg Abbott signed the 2021 state law S.B. 8 banning nearly all abortions, he provided a religious reason as a justification for the law: "Our creator endowed us with the right to life."[49] Kelly Percival questions Abbott's justification, saying, "Whose view of a creator, exactly?"[50] Percival criticizes the legislation and similar movements in other states, writing, "The very problems the First Amendment was designed to avoid—public divisiveness and social conflict based on religious difference—are on full display."[51] Especially, Abbott's signing of the abortion bill underscores the rising influence of the religious right on domestic politics; Abbott has been long supported by the religious right.[52] This is one example of the legislative process and judiciary authority being influenced by the religious right's activism, a trend that raises concern among many about the possible erosion of the principle of separation of church and state.

Originally, as Randall Ballmer argues, one of the religious right's main motives for political activism was to preserve the tax exemptions for segregated Christian schools.[53] However, in their campaign to deny liberal president Jimmy Carter a second term, they strategically seized on the issue of abortion instead because the "anti-abortion crusade was more palatable" than their real motive to protect the segregated schools' tax privilege.[54] In fact, the abortion issue became the critical force to unify theologically varying denominations, bringing together conservative Catholics with conservative Protestants and evangelicals.[55] The religious right's increasing influence wielded through their powerful and sophisticated lobbying and networking infrastructure, which will be elaborated on shortly, has led to the Supreme Court ruling rendered in

June 2022 in the *Dobbs v. Jackson Women's Health Organization* case in favor of state legislature's authority to ban abortion, which overruled the same Court's 1973 *Roe v. Wade* ruling legalizing abortion.

In recent years, the religious right has "invested many hundreds of millions of dollars developing a complex and coordinated infrastructure" including lobbying and networking groups and media.[56] Among others, a critical component of this infrastructure is its "sophisticated legal sphere."[57] For example, the Alliance Defending Freedom, one of the leading organizations in this sphere, is "involved in many of the recent cases intended to degrade the principle of church-state separation."[58] Such organizations have "created a pipeline to funnel ideologues to important judicial positions at the national and federal level."[59] Similarly, the Federalist Society, a major support organization for right-wing jurists, uses the judiciary to push through its agenda, serving "as an enforcement arm of other conservative interests" including the religious right.[60] In fact, as Jonaki Mehta and Courtney Dorning show, the Federalist Society and its leader Leonard Leo, whose "judicial conservatism is deeply rooted in his Catholic" convictions, played an "outsized role" in the efforts to "dismantle Roe v Wade."[61] The Federalist Society has also influenced other Supreme Court decisions on religious agendas such as narrowing the "separation of church and state when it comes to education" in the Court's ruling allowing public financial aid for a Maine-based private school promoting a particular religion.[62] According to Senator Sheldon Whitehouse, as of 2019, nearly 90 percent of President Donald Trump's appellate court nominees were members of the Federalist Society, and all six conservative justices on the Supreme Court were current or former members.[63] The Supreme Court's decision on the 2022 Dobbs case was made in a "6–3 ruling powered by its conservative majority," including conservative Chief Justice John Roberts.[64] According to Reuters's analysis, as of June 2022, twenty-two states were either certain or likely to ban abortion after the *Roe v. Wade* ruling was overturned.[65]

Moreover, the issue of abortion is not the only one that the religious right seeks to address in higher courts by leveraging its relations with justices. As Peter S. Canellos and Josh Gerstein show, leaders of the religious right have extensively lobbied Supreme Court justices such as Clarence Thomas to push through their positions on not only abortion but other agendas such as same-sex rights.[66] Justice Thomas, in his concurrent opinion concerning the *Dobbs* case ruling, urges the Supreme Court to "reconsider" past landmark rulings including protecting the right to contraception and legalizing same-sex marriage nationwide, writing the Court must "correct the error" established in these precedents.[67] According to Lawrence O. Gostin, professor at Georgetown University Law School, now that the majority on the Supreme Court has dismantled the foundation on which the *Roe v. Wade* ruling was built, "the other rights may well come crumbling after."[68]

The religious right's activism, as well as its influence on domestic politics and the judiciary, are weakening the wall between church and state guaranteed under the US Constitution that protects the right to hold religious beliefs of one's choosing and requires the government to remain neutral to different religious denominations. In regard to abortion, there are competing views among and within different denominations, including even among Catholic groups in the United States. For example, as Percival writes, Catholics for Choice advocates for reproductive rights according to the teachings of the Catholic Church while the US Conference of Catholic Bishops interprets those same teachings to describe abortion as an "unspeakable crime."[69] Percival criticizes legislatures and other political leaders who tout religion-based rationales for abortion restrictions as not only disregarding differing convictions among and within many denominations but aiming to "enshrine one narrow theological interpretation into law."[70] She concludes her article by saying, "The First Amendment gives us the right to debate the meaning of life and when it begins. But it also says that such debates have no place in our legislatures or courts of law if we are to be a society that fosters religious freedom for all."[71] While the acceptance of religious elements in the political sphere within the US model of the separation of church and state are capable of reinforcing rather than undermining core democratic values, as discussed in chapter 1, the increasing influence of the religious right on America's legislation and judiciary represents, as Shadi Hamid states, the "danger in transforming mundane political debates into metaphysical questions."[72] Political questions are certainly not metaphysical: they are "of this world and this world alone."[73]

VLADIMIR PUTIN'S RELIGIOUS RHETORIC OF "HOLY RUS" JUSTIFYING HIS WAR IN UKRAINE

Since Russia's military force crossed into Ukraine on February 24, 2022, many have drawn attention to the war's religious dimension, including the close relations between Vladimir Putin's regime and the Russian Orthodox Church.[74] In an address a few days prior to the war, Putin spoke of Ukraine not only as a "neighboring country" but as "an integral part of our own history, culture, and spiritual space."[75] The Russian president has frequently portrayed the invasion as a righteous crusade.[76] He even quoted the Bible in a rally held in Moscow in March 2022, declaring to large crowds, "And this is where the words from the Scripture come to my mind: There is no greater love than if someone gives his soul for his friends."[77] Giles Fraser even describes Putin's war with Ukraine as his "spiritual quest" to rebuild "Christendom, based in Moscow."[78] Whether the Russian president's reference to the religious dimension of the war is genuine or rhetorical is a question that requires further investigation, which this section will pursue.

When Putin declared the commencement of a major military operation in Ukraine in February 2022, he blamed the eastward expansion of the North Atlantic Treaty Organization (NATO) and its "efforts to gain a military foothold of the Ukraine territory" as "unacceptable for [Russia]."[79] He referred to such behaviors as the "policy of containing Russia, with geopolitical dividends," for the United States and its allies. The president further explained that, after "doing everything possible to resolve the situation by peaceful, political means" for "eight endless years," his government had not been left "any other option for defending Russia and our people, other than the one that we are forced to use today."[80] While Western governments and media mostly continue to criticize Putin, there are also many experts, including from the United States and Europe, who have long been warning about the possible consequences of NATO expansion into Eastern Europe. For example, William J. Burns, the Central Intelligence Agency director under the Biden administration, has expressed his concern about the provocative effect of NATO expansion on Russia. A former diplomat, Burns wrote in 2008 in his memo to Secretary of State Condoleezza Rice: "Ukrainian entry into NATO is the brightest of all redlines for the Russian elite (not just Putin)."[81] Ted G. Carpenter critically assesses the US responses to Russia's requests, including those in the few months prior to the execution of Russia's military attack on Ukraine, referring to the period as having "constituted the last chance to avoid a hot war," when the "Kremlin wanted binding assurance that the alliance . . . would never offer membership to Ukraine."[82] The Biden administration's response to Russia's quest was, Carpenter writes, "tepid and evasive" and then Putin "clearly decided to escalate matters."[83] Thus, Putin's decision to wage war with Ukraine was geopolitical in nature.

Furthermore, historical analysis of Putin's period in power by John Anderson demonstrates no serious state-led attempt to restore the political authority of the Russian Orthodox Church, and religious matters are basically "secondary affairs at the Kremlin, except where they impinge on security or social harmony."[84] Although the president has made regular visits to church services and pilgrimage sites during his period in office, the "precise nature of his religious faith is less certain" and "there is little evidence that Putin's thinking is fundamentally influenced by a theological perspective."[85]

The marginality of religion for the Putin administration, however, should not be interpreted as suggesting that the president has not highlighted the importance of the roles that religion can play. In fact, he has emphasized the importance of religion in terms of its securitization. A Russian government document approved by presidential decree in 2000 called for the protection of Russia's national security including, unusually for a national security document, the "preservation of the cultural, spiritual, and moral heritage" and "resistance to the negative influence of foreign religious organizations and missionaries."[86] This tendency to see foreign religious organizations as a threat is shared by the leadership of the Russian Orthodox Church, whose position is shaped by a "view of national belonging and a pragmatic desire to constrain the activities of religious competitors."[87] As Anderson argues, the talk of "universal values," characteristics of the Gorbachev and Yeltsin years, "has disappeared."[88] Instead, religion is linked to nationalism. The Russian Orthodox Church leadership and the president share a "common view of the need to restore Russian greatness and sense of nationhood, as well as the Church's feeling that the securitization of religion may strengthen their argument for recognition as the church of the nation."[89]

With his background in the KGB during the Soviet era, Putin is a pragmatic and realistic politician who is committed to the mission of protecting and strengthening the state of Russia. With respect to the religious sphere of Russia's war with Ukraine, Geraldine Fagan writes, "For Vladimir Putin, Orthodox Christianity is a tool for asserting Moscow's rights over sovereign Ukraine."[90] Thus, Putin's approach to religion is motivated by his belief in the need for spiritual coherence and the reinforcement of Russian security, to the extent that it contributes to his overall mission of restoring Russia as a great world power.

THE CASE OF JAPAN

There is a significant difference between the history of Japan and the West from a religious perspective. For instance, up to the modern period, Japan lacked independent religious institutions with the authority to critique political power holders. Religious groups were under the control of secular authorities as the power holders simply forced Buddhist and other religious institutions to submit whenever they found the doctrines or practices of these religions to be inconvenient. In the West, on the other hand, the major Christian churches, with their universal values, competed with secular authorities who represented merely local political ones. Therefore, transcendent religiosity, for all its problems, has developed in the West, while Japan lags behind due to its state-centric political culture.

Partly as a result of this history, modern Japan has not had access to the positive concept of religion distinct from the state. As Jason Josephson argues throughout his book *The Invention of Religion in Japan*, the country to some degree "invented" the category of religion at the end of the nineteenth century in the process of becoming a modern nation-state. Indeed, *shūkyō* (religion) was a new word in Japanese in this period.[91] Thus, secularization did not go hand in hand with modernization in Japan, as opposed to the cases in Western Europe and elsewhere. In the Soviet Union, for example, secularization and even atheization were key elements of the government's modernization drive, as discussed in chapter 1.

This lack of a publicly available universal religious perspective that might shape or critique the activity of state politics had profound consequences for Japan in the twentieth century. For example, throughout World War II, Japanese authorities invented a narrow veneration of the emperor in a form generally called State Shinto.[92] Furthermore, organized religions were neutralized by the state unless they fully supported the country's war efforts by embracing State Shinto, which highlights a significant difference from the religious competition in Western Europe. In fact, the situation was so extreme that modern Japan was a true theocracy with the emperor as the head of state and also a living deity. Similar setups may be found in the Imperial Cult of the ancient Roman Empire, where the emperors and their families were worshiped as divine.[93] Another example would be the Ptolemaic Cult of Alexander the Great, where the deification of Alexander was used to rule the Ptolemaic Kingdom, the ancient Greek state based in Egypt.[94] However, both of these examples are found thousands of years in the past. No such equivalents to the Japanese theocracy are found at this same time in history; other countries may have coopted religion for their goals, but not in this exact way. Such an arrangement made religion the pawn of politics rather than a perspective from which to criticize and inform politics, as would be the case in a genuine democracy. Moreover, this religious system was deeply interconnected with Japan's foreign policy and fueled the country's increased aggression against other countries including Korea, China, Russia, and the United States, leading to World War II. This arrangement was dissolved with Japan's defeat in the war through the Occupation Authority's political reorientation.

After the war, Japan struggled, and continues to struggle, to see democratic politics as a process informed by a universal vision of good rather than as merely a struggle between power holders. The experience of Japanese people in reconciling religiopolitical interests has naturally much in common with that in other societies, but the uniqueness of its historical, political, and religious context makes it a rich topic for further exploration.

CONCLUSION

The case studies discussed in this chapter have provided perspectives on the state and religion relations in different countries. They have also demonstrated the possibility of both positive and negative influence of religion on politics as well as how religions could be exploited by the state authorities and power holders.

In the following chapters, I will explore a discussion on the relevance of religious perspectives to the Japanese political landscape and on the country's unique state-religion dynamics in the periods extending from premodern and modern to contemporary times. By doing so, the discussion will examine the problematic developments in Japan, including during the extreme militaristic phase and the more recent economistic phase, providing insights for a better understanding of the political culture of the country and implications for addressing global challenges.

NOTES

1. David F. Schmitz and Vanessa Walker, "Jimmy Carter and the Foreign Policy of Human Rights: The Development of a Post-Cold War Foreign Policy," *Diplomatic History* 28, no. 1 (2004): 117, http://www.jstor.org/stable/24914773 (May 15, 2023).

2. William Steding, *Presidential Faith and Foreign Policy* (London: Palgrave Macmillan, 2014), 40.

3. Friedbert Pflüger, "Human Rights Unbound: Carter's Human Rights Policy Reassessed," *Presidential Studies Quarterly* 19, no. 4 (1989): 705–16, http://www.jstor.org/stable/27550568 (May 15, 2023).

4. Schmitz and Walker, "Jimmy Carter," 120.

5. Schmitz and Walker, "Jimmy Carter," 114.

6. Zbigniew Brzezinski, *Power and Principle* (Toronto: McGraw-Hill Ryerson, 1983), 460.

7. Brzezinski, *Power and Principle*, 124.

8. Schmitz and Walker, "Jimmy Carter," 114 and 137.

9. Schmitz and Walker, "Jimmy Carter," 138.

10. Schmitz and Walker, "Jimmy Carter," 139.

11. Brzezinski, *Power and Principle*, 128.

12. Brzezinski, *Power and Principle*, 128–29.

13. Brzezinski, Power and Principle, 397.

14. Brzezinski, Power and Principle, 354.

15. John Gilbert, "Jimmy Carter's Human Rights Policy and Iran: A Reexamination," *Madison Historical Review* 5, Article 1 (2014): 23. https://commons.lib.jmu.edu/mhr/vol5/iss1/1/ (September 18, 2023).

16. Brzezinski, *Power and Principle*, 49.

17. Brzezinski, *Power and Principle*, 49.

18. Jimmy Carter, *Faith: A Journey for All* (New York: Simon & Schuster, 2018), 56–57.

19. Jimmy Carter, *Inaugural Address of President Jimmy Carter*, January 20, 1977, https://www.jimmycarterlibrary.gov/assets/documents/speeches/inaugadd.phtml (May 9, 2023).

20. Cited in David Shaw, "Jimmy Carter's Rise Brought Evangelicalism to the Front Pages," *Los Angeles Times*, December 28, 1983, 16.

21. Carter, *Faith*, 57.

22. Carter, *Faith*, 42–43.

23. Stephen Rock, *Faith and Foreign Policy* (London: Bloomsbury Publishing, 2011), 38.

24. Rock, *Faith and Foreign Policy.*

25. Carter, *Faith*, 91.

26. Carter, *Faith*, 101.

27. Carter, *Faith*, 92.

28. Carter, *Faith*, 92.

29. Pflüger, "Human Rights," 705.

30. Pflüger, "Human Rights," 705.

31. Schmitz and Walker, "Jimmy Carter," 143.

32. Schmitz and Walker, "Jimmy Carter," 143.

33. David Dumke, "P-I Focus: Bush Weds Religion, Politics to Form World View," *Seattle Post-Intelligencer*, August 21, 2004, https://www.seattlepi.com/local/opinion/article/P-I-Focus-Bush-weds-religion-politics-to-form-1152104.php (May 10, 2023).

34. Dumke, "Bush Weds Religion, Politics."

35. Jim Wallis, "Dangerous Religion: George W. Bush's Theology of Empire," *Mississippi Review* 32, no. 3 (2004): 60–72, http://www.jstor.org/stable/20132445.

36. Wallis, "Dangerous Religion," 60–72.

37. Wallis, "Dangerous Religion," 60–72.

38. Ewen MacAskill, "George Bush: 'God Told Me to End the Tyranny in Iraq,'" *Guardian*, 7 Oct. 2005, https://www.theguardian.com/world/2005/oct/07/iraq.usa (10 May 2023).

39. Cited in MacAskill, "George Bush."

40. Pew Research Center, "Religious Groups Issue Statements on War with Iraq," comp. Religion News Service, March 19, 2003, https://www.pewresearch.org/religion/2003/03/19/publicationpage-aspxid616/ (May 10, 2023).

41. Ed Vulliamy, "Iraq War 'Unjustifiable' Says Bush's Church Head," *Guardian*, October 20, 2002, https://www.theguardian.com/world/2002/oct/20/usa.iraq (May 10, 2023).

42. United Methodist Communications, "Church Executive Urges Bush Not to Attack Iraq," press release, September 3, 2002, https://archive.wfn.org/2002/09/msg00033.html (May 10, 2023).

43. United Methodist Communications, "Church Executive Urges Bush."

44. Richard Falk, *Declining World Order* (New York: Routledge, 2004), 189–90.

45. Falk, *Declining World Order*, 191.

46. Falk, *Declining World Order*, 192.

47. Dumke, "Bush Weds Religion, Politics."

48. Brigitte P. Volochinsky, "The Bush Presidency: Undermining the Separation Between Church and State," Inquiries Journal 2, no. 7 (2010), http://www.inquiriesjournal.com/articles/266/the-bush-presidency-undermining-the-separation-between-church-and-state (May 10, 2023).

49. Cited in Shannon Najmabadi, "Gov. Greg Abbott Signs into Law One of Nation's Strictest Abortion Measures, Banning Procedure as Early as Six Weeks into a Pregnancy," *Texas Tribune*, May 19, 2021, https://www.texastribune.org/2021/05/18/texas-heartbeat-bill-abortions-law/ (May 10, 2023).

50. Kelly Percival, "Religion Must Not Substitute Science in the Abortion Debate," *Brennan Center for Justice at NYU Law*, November 5, 2021, https://www.brennancenter.org/our-work/analysis-opinion/religion-must-not-substitute-science-abortion-debate (May 10, 2023).

51. Percival, "Abortion Debate."

52. Texas Freedom Network, "Group Prepares to Anoint Greg Abbott as Religious Right's Favored Candidate in Texas Governor's Race," *Texas Freedom Network Blog*, March 11, 2014, https://tfn.org/group-prepares-to-anoint-greg-abbott-as-religious-rights-favored-candidate-in-texas-governors-race/ (May 10, 2023).

53. Randall Balmer, "The Real Origin of the Religious Right," *Politico Magazine*, May 27, 2014, https://www.politico.com/magazine/story/2014/05/religious-right-real-origins-107133/ (May 10, 2023).

54. Balmer, "Religious Right."

55. Katherine Stewart, "How the Christian Right Took over the Judiciary and Changed America," *Guardian*, June 25, 2022, https://www.theguardian.com/world/2022/jun/25/roe-v-wade-abortion-christian-right-america (May 10, 2023).

56. Stewart, "Christian Right."

57. Stewart, "Christian Right."

58. Stewart, "Christian Right."

59. Stewart, "Christian Right."

60. Christopher Rhodes, "The Federalist Society: Architects of the American Dystopia," *Al Jazeera*, June 29, 2022, https://www.aljazeera.com/opinions

/2022/6/29/the-federalist-society-architects-of-the-american-dystopia (May 10, 2023).

61. Jonaki Mehta and Courtney Dorning, "One Man's Outsized Role in Shaping the Supreme Court and Overturning Roe," *NPR*, June 20, 2022, https://www.npr.org/2022/06/30/1108351562/roe-abortion-supreme-court-scotus-law (May 10, 2023).

62. Rhodes, "The Federalist Society."

63. Sheldon Whitehouse, "The Third Federalist Society," speech presented March 27, 2019, https://www.whitehouse.senate.gov/news/speeches/the-third-federalist-society (May 10, 2023).

64. Lawrence Hurley and Andrew Chung, "U.S. Supreme Court Overturns Roe v. Wade, Ends Constitutional Right to Abortion," *Reuters*, June 28, 2022, https://www.reuters.com/world/us/us-supreme-court-overturns-abortion-rights-landmsark-2022-06-24/ (May 10, 2023).

65. Reuters, "Abortion Access in a Post-Roe America," *Reuters Graphics*, June 24, 2022, https://graphics.reuters.com/USA-ABORTION/GRAPHIC/zgpomdbeopd/index.html (May 10, 2023).

66. Peter S. Canellos and Josh Gerstein, "'Operation Higher Court': Inside the Religious Right's Efforts to Wine and Dine Supreme Court Justices," *Politico*, July 8, 2022, https://www.politico.com/news/2022/07/08/religious-right-supreme-court-00044739 (May 10, 2023).

67. Clarence Thomas, "Justice Thomas' Concurring Opinion on Thomas E. Dobbs, State Health Officer of the Mississippi Department of Health, et al., Petitioners v. Jackson Women's Health Organization, et al," 597 US (2022), no. 19–1392, June 24, 2022, *Supreme Court of Justice of the United States syllabus*, October Term 2021, https://www.supremecourt.gov/opinions/21pdf/19-1392_6j37.pdf (May 10, 2023).

68. Cited in Sheryl Gay Stolberg, "Thomas's Concurring Opinion Raises Questions About What Rights Might Be Next," *New York Times*, June 24, 2022, https://www.nytimes.com/2022/06/24/us/clarence-thomas-roe-griswold-lawrence-obergefell.html (May 10, 2023).

69. Percival, "Abortion Debate."

70. Percival, "Abortion Debate."

71. Percival, "Abortion Debate."

72. Shadi Hamid, "America Without God," *Atlantic*, March 10, 2021, https://www.theatlantic.com/magazine/archive/2021/04/america-politics-religion/618072/ (May 10, 2023).

73. Hamid, "America Without God."

74. European Parliament Think Tank, "Russia's War on Ukraine: The Religious Dimension," April 1, 2022, https://www.europarl.europa.eu/RegData/etudes/ATAG/2022/729355/EPRS_ATA(2022)729355_EN.pdf (May 11, 2023).

75. Vladimir Putin, "Address by the President of the Russian Federation," *Official Internet Resources of the President of Russia*, February 21, 2022, http://en.kremlin.ru/events/president/news/67828 (May 11, 2023).

76. Knox Thames, "Putin's Unholy War," *Atlantic Council: UkraineAlert* (blog), April 22, 2022, https://www.atlanticcouncil.org/blogs/ukrainealert/putins-unholy-war/ (May 11, 2023).

77. Vladimir Putin, "'Those Storms Will Contribute to Russia's Glory': Putin Quotes National Hero to Packed Stadium" (speech), *NBC News*, March 19, 2022, https://www.nbcnews.com/video/at-huge-rally-putin-uses-bible-and-russian-history-to-justify-ukraine-invasion-135721541797 (May 11, 2023).

78. Giles Fraser, "Putin's Spiritual Destiny," The London School of Economics and Political Science Religion and Global Society Blog, February 25, 2022, https://blogs.lse.ac.uk/religionglobalsociety/2022/02/putins-spiritual-destiny/ (May 11, 2023).

79. Vladimir Putin, "Address by the President of the Russian Federation," *Official Internet Resources of the President of Russia*, February 24, 2022, http://en.kremlin.ru/events/president/news/67843 (May 11, 2023).

80. Putin, "Address," February 24, 2022.

81. Quoted in US Congress, *Congressional Record*, February 10, 2022, vol. 168, issue 27, https://www.govinfo.gov/app/details/CREC-2022-02-10 (May 11, 2023).

82. Ted G. Carpenter, "Many Predicted NATO Expansion Would Lead to War. Those Warnings Were Ignored," *Guardian*, February 28, 2022, https://www.theguardian.com/commentisfree/2022/feb/28/nato-expansion-war-russia-ukraine (May 11, 2023).

83. Carpenter, "NATO Expansion."

84. John Anderson, "Putin and the Russian Orthodox Church: Asymmetric Symphonia?" *Journal of International Affairs* 61, no. 1 (Fall/Winter 2007): 186, http://www.jstor.org/stable/24358086 (May 11, 2023).

85. Anderson, "Putin," 188.

86. Russian Government, "National Security Concept of the Russian Federation," *Medzinárodné Otázky* 9, no. 3 (2000): 112, http://www.jstor.org/stable/44963336 (May 11, 2023).

87. Anderson, "Putin," 195.

88. Anderson, "Putin," 195.

89. Anderson, "Putin," 195.

90. Geraldine Fagan, "How the Russian Orthodox Church Is Helping Drive Putin's War in Ukraine," Time, April 25, 2022, https://time.com/6167332/putin-russian-orthodox-church-war-ukraine/ (May 11, 2023).

91. Jason Josephson, *The Invention of Religion in Japan* (Chicago: University of Chicago Press, 2012).

92. There has been scholarly debate revolving around the term and concept of "State Shinto." For a summary of the debate, see Helen Hardacre, *Shinto: A History* (New York: Oxford University Press, 2017), 355–57.

93. Religion and Public Life, "Cult of Emperor," n.d., https://rpl.hds.harvard.edu/faq/cult-emperor (May 11, 2023).

94. Lily Ross Taylor, "The Cult of Alexander at Alexandria," *Classical Philology* 22, no. 2 (April 1927): 162–69, http://www.jstor.org/stable/263514 (May 11, 2023).

Chapter 3

Transcendence and the State

Japanese Religion from the Early Modern Period to the Nineteenth Century

In the early modern period prior to the Meiji Restoration of 1868, religions were essentially subordinated to the state, resultantly creating a secular civilization as will be discussed in the course of this chapter. At the same time, modern Japan's government, which seized power by overthrowing the Tokugawa government of feudal Japan and terminating the country's isolation from the rest of the world, was faced with a pressing urgency to integrate and build a state quickly. It eventually sought to achieve this by centralizing authority in the state and the emperor. Specifically, the government demanded from its people secular as well as religious loyalty to the emperor, using ancient Japanese mythology to deify him and create the religious ideology of State Shinto. Although the post-Meiji Restoration period of rapid industrialization is often compared to Western Europe's period of modernization, Japan's modernization was founded on a significantly different principle of state building in terms of the relationship between state and religion. While in Western Europe the nation-state was built upon the secularity of the state, or the separation of church and state, modern Japan took a rather complex direction in this regard.

This chapter will explore state-religion relations in Japan after 1608, explaining the nature of the relationships that existed in Japan and the mutual hostility between religious institutions and the state. The chapter will also review Japan's state-religion relations toward the end of the early modern period, with a focus on the standpoints of the country unifiers and the Tokugawa government. It will then examine in more detail the country's state-religion relations in the modern period.

STATE AND RELIGION IN EARLY MODERN JAPAN

State-religion relations in the early modern period in Japan stood in contrast to those in Europe prior to the modern period. In Western Europe, until medieval times, papal authority competed with or even exceeded secular authority in influence, underpinning the formation of civilization. In Japan, on the other hand, no religious authority had developed that could compete with secular authority, and secular authority was always superior to religious authority.

In his 2017 article on premodern secularism, Kiri Paramore argued that the Japanese capital stabilized between 794 and 1185, in a period that would be best described as the first *longue durée* in Japan. During this period, Japan established institutional practices that both linked and differentiated the Buddhist monasteries and the imperial court. The settled regime of the imperial government and the Buddhist monasteries maintained a stable relationship of understanding and respect up to the fifteenth century. This situation was different from that in Europe, where the Church was in constant conflict with secular kings as each side sought to have executive power.[1] The comparably stable environment in Japan facilitated the institutionalization of politicoreligious relations through interactions between the aristocratic networks that represented secular states and Buddhist clerical institutions such as the *sangha.* The practices that enhanced the stable interaction of these institutions included family relations between members of aristocratic institutions and Buddhist clerical institutions; the movement of people between the institutions, such as the retirement of noble secular leaders into monasteries; and the participation of each in the other's activity, such as the participation in regime wars and Buddhist prayers by both parties. It is intriguing to note that the rise of the warrior *shogunal* government after the collapse of court rule did not interrupt the pattern—rather, the same interaction patterns were incorporated by the ruling *Kamakura samurai* nobility.

The medieval to early modernist period in Japan saw a dramatic transition where the long-lasting state-religion relationship was interrupted. This transition was met with fifteenth- and sixteenth-century movements by rebellious and autonomous groups that sought to change the way in which religious and political institutions governed society. The rebellious groups proposed broader renewed visions that would change the old religious and political institutionalism and alter the existing relationship between worldly status and power. Where Europe had some dynamic movements such as Lutheranism, Japan had *ikkō ikki*, peasant communities that were federated and that arose as groups independent from the warrior ruling class of *samurai* lords. In his book *Japanese Warrior Monks AD 949–1603*, Stephen Turnbull contends that *ikkō ikki* groups arose around the fifteenth and sixteenth centuries and were identified by their shared belief in True Pure Land Buddhism.[2] Together with other peasant groups, they were commonly referred to as *ikki* and orchestrated most local revolts in the country. They can be paralleled with Lutheran reformism that disengaged from religious institutionalism.

The history of state conflicts that entwined with religion can be described better from the negative perspective of Oda Nobunaga and Toyotomi Hideyoshi, known as "unifiers" of early modern Japan, in their country-unifying process in the late sixteenth century directed toward Buddhism. Oda Nobunaga used his superior military strength to brutally suppress the *ikkō ikki* forces in a bid to unify a huge region of Japan. One should recall that Buddhism and secular government in Japan had a special relationship, as the secular leaders often interacted with and participated in Buddhist practices while the Buddhist leaders supported the efforts of the secular law. Yet unifiers such as Nobunaga saw Buddhism as a threat to unification because it served as a spiritual driver of the *ikkō ikki* leadership.[3] Consequently, Nobunaga did not show any mercy to Buddhist leaders, a move that was often viewed as hostility toward the religion itself. Nobunaga, viewing Buddhism as an obstacle to the country's unification, attacked Hongan-ji temple, which had supported the True Pure Land followers' protest, and in 1571 destroyed towns and temples in the Mount Hiei area that had been regarded as symbols of Buddhist authority.[4]

The unifiers' hostile stance toward these religious communities and authorities also stemmed ideologically from their antagonism to Buddhist transcendency and absolutism. Satō Hiroo, referring to Nobunaga's furious attack on the Mount Hiei area, writes, "Nobunaga's actions speak more eloquently than anything else of the nature of early modern powerholders, who refuse to recognize any authority that exceeds or rivals their own, and seek to bring even religious authority to its knees at their own feet."[5]

Speaking of religious transcendency, Maruyama Masao describes Buddhism as "a world religion that introduced a completely new spiritual dimension to the Japanese."[6] He emphasizes its essentially transcendent nature in relation to secular authorities. Referring to the Seventeen-Article Constitution issued by Prince Shōtoku Taishi in AD 604 that emphasized Buddhist principles that the secular authorities should respect, Maruyama argues that "the idea contained here is that any authorities on the earth, including political authorities, should be subordinate to and serve the universal truth or universal norm: that what is stipulated by the authority is not the truth or justice, and that the authority is not identified with the truth."[7] Although Maruyama recognizes various changes in Buddhism's sociopolitical position throughout the history of Japan,[8] he stresses the significance of its transcendent orientation that provided an unprecedented perspective to the Japanese, in contrast to more conventional doctrines such as Confucianism that were basically incorporated into the secular state system. Maruyama states that "preaching devotion to a particular religion called Buddhism is not the point here. The important point here is that devotion to it was recognized as devotion to an absolute and universal value."[9]

Transcendent orientations were also highlighted by new schools of Buddhism that were founded during the Kamakura period (1185–1333), including those founded by Nichiren and Hōnen. Nichiren emphasized the significance of the Lotus Sutra, one of the most influential teachings of Siddhārtha Gautama, as the way for individuals to attain enlightenment. He encouraged his followers to sustain their faith even before the demand from the state authority to abandon their faith, referring to the power holders of Japan as the "rulers of this little island."[10] Maruyama stresses the frequent citation by Nichiren of the Buddhist concept "rely on the dharma, and not on the person," as it demonstrates Nichiren's standpoint of "making the truths of the Lotus Sutra, the universal, the only behavioral criteria that are not affected by earthly personal or power relations."[11] Hōnen taught faith in Amida Buddha as a transcendent being, abstracting Buddhism from worldly affairs. It is no coincidence that the aforementioned protests from Buddhist communities against the unifiers emerged from these new schools of Buddhism. As Satō says, although these protest movements were "regarded as heretical by the schools' mainstream," they were characterized "with independence and transcendency superseding the worldly authority" that was inherent in the teachings of Nichiren and Hōnen.[12] The independence and transcendency shown by these movements fueled the tensions between religious institutions and the secular power holders, the unifiers in this case.

The unifiers outlawed and suppressed Christianity, too, because it showed signs of transcendence and absolutism. Although it had been tolerated for some time since having been introduced to Japan in the mid-sixteenth century, the unifiers realized that the religion seemed to provide no advantage to the secular authority and its goals. This can be attributed to the nature of Christianity from the West. George Holmes argues that the realization of how the Catholic Church was structured and the struggle for power between the Church and the secular government discouraged Japanese power holders from supporting Christianity.[13] Hideyoshi regarded the gradually growing Christian religion as a threat and issued an edict in 1596 banning the propagation of Christianity. He also executed twenty-six Catholic missionaries and local lay followers in 1597. These suppressions of religions demonstrate, as Satō puts it, the "characteristic of the unifiers in the early modern period that did not recognize any authority that is superior or equal to themselves and sought to have the religious authorities kneel down at their feet."[14] Thus, the unifiers deprived the potentially independent religions of their influence.

RELIGIOUS CONTROL UNDER THE TOKUGAWA GOVERNMENT

For the Tokugawa government that succeeded the unifiers, the issue of how to incorporate religion into its political power system remained a major issue. The ruling classes in this period more often than not saw Christianity as a competitor and a threat to their authority. As cited by Hiyane Antei (1942, 134), the Tokugawa government issued Shūmon

Torishimari Kisoku (Sect Control Regulations) in 1613, which listed both Christianity and the fuju-fuse sect of the Nichiren School of Buddhism as "heretical teachings."[15] Compared to Nobunaga, who had merely prohibited the propagation of Christianity, the Tokugawa government tightened control over Christianity from 1611 by banning practice of it as well. Furthermore, by issuing a national seclusion order in 1639, the government severed its relations with Western countries like Portugal that had dispatched missionaries. Though part of the objective of the seclusion policy was to deter the political and economic influence of Western powers, it also sought to exclude Christianity in particular. Maruyama emphasizes the need to "understand the issue of prohibition of Christianity as part of the significant historical incident toward the complete subordination of religion to the secular authority in the process of the foundation of the early modern control system."[16] As Maruyama argues, the banning of Christianity represented the denial of any authority superior to the secular authority.

Helen Hardacre also indicates the shift in relations between religious institutions and the government by referring to regulations issued by secular leadership to the major temples, demanding their incorporation of strict measures to regulate monks and occupy themselves with doctrinal study.[17] As a result, a system of controlling and administrating religious institutions was introduced by the mid-seventeenth century. The system was based on four main principles: (1) absolutely prohibiting Christianity (this was achieved through full suppression of the Shimabara Rebellion in 1637; the ban was also enforced through annual sectarian investigation that determined whether people were registered to Buddhism or Christianity); (2) incorporating all Buddhist clerics and temples into predetermined sects that were governed by rigid rules; (3) incorporating the whole population of Japan into Buddhist temples; and (4) placing the management of shrine affairs under the Yoshida house.[18]

Another main target of the Tokugawa government's religious repression was a small subschool of the Nichiren School of Buddhism, the fuju-fuse sect led by the priest Nichiō, which refused obedience to the secular authority. The power holders exiled Nichiō and other leaders of the sect and executed several of them. The strong degree of suppression of this relatively minor sect demonstrates the Tokugawa government's sensitivity to any religion that indicated an independent orientation.

Another major approach adopted by the Tokugawa government after 1635 to control religion was the introduction of the mandatory danka, a kind of parishioner system that made it compulsory for every individual and family to be registered with a Buddhist temple. Primarily intended to detect Christians and followers of the fuju-fuse sect of the Nichiren School of Buddhism, the danka system had temples issue terauke shōmon, or temple registration certificates, to prove affiliation, which were then collected by local authorities to prepare shūmon ninbetsuchō, the religious census. Furthermore, the system, which started with individual and family-based registration, later required registration by neighborhood groups called gonin gumi, or a five-household unit. In other words, registration and affiliation with a particular Buddhist temple served administrative control purposes that had nothing to do with individuals' own faith.

Under the danka system, the conventional Buddhist sects were reorganized and incorporated into the Tokugawa government's control system, which left virtually no room for other religions to survive. As Tamamuro Fumio describes, because the monks of the temples played the "roles of junior officers serving their local feudal lord," the danka system "significantly deprived them of faith-based motivation for propagation."[19] Thus, Buddhism in Japan was turned into so-called sōshiki bukkyō, or funeral Buddhism, where monks only provided funeral and other related services for their affiliated "followers," losing the essential qualities of independence and transcendence.

Although the danka system helped Buddhist temples grow significantly in terms of the number of supposed followers, the Buddhism propagated under the system obviously did not develop transcendent or independent values among people. On the contrary, as Satō describes, Buddhism played the "role of religiously legitimating obedience to the authority and aggregating people under the authority."[20]

The Tokugawa government, which lasted over 260 years, reinforced Japan's political intolerance of religions with a transcendent or independent orientation by disempowering Buddhism and Christianity and isolating the country from the rest of the world through its national seclusion policy. Thus, in contrast to Western Europe, where religion (namely Christianity) competed with or even had an influence superior to that of secular authority, Japan's religion-state relations prior to the modern period were established in a fundamentally different relationship. The relationship between the state and religion varied depending on the secular leadership that existed at the time. Some religions were strongly opposed because they were considered a threat. At times, leaders subordinated, dominated, and used religions to their own advantage.[21]

The previous examples of the early modern treatment of religion highlight the differences between Japan and early modern Europe discussed in the preceding chapter. Church and state in Europe were, to some degree, evenly matched partners and opponents—partners insofar as they joined forces to administer society, and opponents insofar as they sought to encroach on each other's territory. By contrast, Japan's various faith traditions and devotional communities never had an equivalent role in administering society because they had no comparable administrative authority. They sometimes wielded a spiritual influence, but their bureaucratic shape was largely controlled by the state.

STATE AND RELIGION DURING THE MODERN STATE-BUILDING PERIOD

Following the overthrow of the Tokugawa government that began Japan's modern period, the new government of Meiji, which seized power with imperial legitimation under the Decree for the Restoration of Imperial Rule, was faced with pressing urgency to build its power base and cope with external pressures. To this end, it sought to restore the emperor's authority based on ancient mythology.

Elevating Shinto to a de Facto State Religion

The imperial mythology was created for political means around the early eighth century by order of the ancient imperial court in the form of mystical written histories of Japan, including *Nihon Shoki* (Chronicle of Japan) and *Kojiki* (Record of Ancient Matters), which described emperors as descendants of deities and thereby divinized them. *Nihon Shoki* and *Kojiki* also introduced the notion of Shinto, literally meaning "the way of deities," as a traditional religion of Japan to support the emperor's divinity. In actuality, prior to the eighth century there did not exist such a religion that could be defined with a single term, but rather a mixture of folk beliefs and rituals, many of which were a kind of animism or related to Buddhism.[22] There was no single Japanese "religion" called Shinto in ancient Japan,[23] but rather a set of overlapping devotional practices.

Furthermore, the emperor was not only divinized but also played the role of a shaman. In this sense, the cult of the emperor was a form of magical manipulation rather than worship of deities, corresponding to what Max Weber referred to as "coercion of the god," where the shaman was "stronger even than the god."[24] In fact, the emperor, who was considered to be simultaneously a living deity and shaman, was positioned to be superior to other deities, as indicated by the use of the term *tennō* or heavenly sovereign to refer to the emperor. Originating from Daoism, this term refers to the highest-ranking deity among deities. In Japan, this term has been applied to the human emperor, indicating that the earthly authority has been positioned as superior to the deities.[25] Implying sole, absolute authority over its people, this position of the emperor is unparalleled even by theocratic leaders of other civilizations, such as those in premodern Europe, where the earthly authority was legitimated by, but not considered equal or superior to, the higher being. Although the imperial court's influence weakened during the medieval and early modern periods, the position of the emperor indicates a prototype of Japan's religion-state relations, where the earthly authority is positioned as superior to the heavenly authority.

In the nineteenth century, the government sought to establish its power base by allocating political, military, and religious authority to the emperor based on restoring the ancient precedent of *saisei icchi*, or the unity of religious rites and government.[26] The new government was not only focused on transforming power from Tokugawa's samurai leadership but also on establishing a theocracy that was based on the idea of the divinity of an emperor. This was the main standing point from which forces of nationalism were developed. Such changes elevated Shinto to the position of Japan's de facto state religion.

During the adoption of Shinto as a state religion, the government set up the *Jingikan*, or the Department of Divinity, to place all Shinto shrines throughout Japan under its control. The duties of the *Jingikan* included recruiting official missionaries and propagating the state religion among the people. In 1871, the government ordered the confiscation of most of the lands that had been owned by shrines and temples in exchange for a provision of rice, depriving those establishments of their economic autonomy and replacing it with dependence on the state. Furthermore, the government forbade the traditional hereditary succession of Shinto priests and replaced it with a policy of governmental appointment of priests. Thus, Shinto shrines with origins too diverse to be grouped under a single homogenous religion were nevertheless reorganized and institutionalized as part of the state religion system. The government also declared the abolition of the Buddhist temple-based *danka* system developed under the Tokugawa government and instead commenced the *ujiko* or shrine parishioner system, which sought to have all people in Japan registered with local Shinto shrines to accelerate the implementation of its *saisei icchi* policy.

Changing Government Stance on Christianity and Buddhism

The transcendent nature of Christianity was in direct conflict with the government's standpoint of divinizing and absolutizing the emperor and denying any religious or secular authority that would compete with or be superior to him or the state. The government banned Christianity, including cracking down on the Christian community in the Urakami village, Nagasaki, in 1870 by sending over three thousand people into exile in various parts of the country.

The government also sought to undermine Buddhism. Although Buddhism had long lost its essential transcendent orientation under the early modern period's *danka* system, it had maintained a stable presence partly owing to that very system. In fact, many Shinto shrines had been under the influence of, or even subordinated to, Buddhism, including enshrining Buddhist statues such as those of popular Boddhisattva Hachiman as their objects of worship and allowing themselves to be run by Buddhist monks. Some Shintoists also undermined Buddhism with the accusation that Buddhist priests did not support the government's invasion and control of other countries such as China. Seeking to reverse the positions of the two religions and promote Shinto as a distinct religion, Japan's government in March 1868 issued the Edict on the Separation of Shinto and Buddhism, instructing Shinto shrines to remove statues of Buddha.[27] A month later, the government issued another notification to change the title given to *Hachiman* from the

Great Bodhisattva to the Great Deity. In the following year, it ordered Buddhist monks running Shinto shrines either to become Shinto priests or to leave the shrines.

The policy to rid Shinto of Buddhist influence triggered an anti-Buddhist movement among Shinto priests who were appointed government officials, in many cases having long been subordinated to Buddhist monks. The movement turned fierce in many areas, with Shinto priests bursting into Buddhist temples and arbitrarily removing and throwing away Buddha statues and other articles, forcing Buddhist monks to abandon their temples and become farmers. Although the government issued a notification for Shinto priests to refrain from excessively aggressive actions, it rarely interfered with them and allowed the situation to develop as it did. The movement was mainly led by leaders of conventional feudal domains and lasted for around three years until the nation's centralization was completed with the implementation of *haihan-chiken*, the abolition of feudal domains and establishment of prefectures, in 1871.

The implementation of *haihan-chiken* marked the termination of the feudal system that had developed throughout the medieval and early modern periods, and the establishment of the centralized government system of modern Japan. By 1873, the government had also lifted the ban on Christianity and discontinued the statutory registration of Shinto parishioners. This shift also reflected the need for the government to prioritize economic development and external relations, leading it to make a drastic policy change vis-à-vis religion. Excluding Buddhism was deemed unrealistic given its long-established relations with communities of people, regardless of the fact that these relationships might not necessarily be faith based, while foreign pressures made legalizing Christianity inevitable.

At the same time, the shift in religious policy reflected the government's intention to use not only Shinto but all other religions, too, for the purpose of state building. In 1872, the government abolished the Ministry (formerly Department) of Divinity and instead set up *Kyōbu-shō*, or the Ministry of Religious Education, seeking to "educate" people and teach them nationalist ideals based on the imperial system by mobilizing all religions. To the same end, the Shinto missionary system was terminated and instead a *kōdō-shoku* or evangelist system was introduced, appointing not only Shinto priests but also Buddhist monks and other individuals as evangelists. In the same year, the government issued a notification allowing Buddhist monks to eat meat and get married, going against the tradition of most of the Buddhist schools as well as rules set by the Tokugawa government. This move sought to manipulate Buddhist monks into serving the state by deliberately having them deviate from their religious doctrines and the rules established under the feudal system. In fact, most Buddhist monks accepted the government's dispensation.[28] Additionally, the Ministry of Religious Education requested each school of Buddhism designate a *kanchō* or superintendent priest, seeking to manage religion efficiently in order to promote nationalistic education.

On the other hand, the government banned new religions that emerged in the early modern and modern periods, such as Tenrikyō and Konkōkyō, whose doctrines lacked conformity with emperor worship. Facing the threat of extinction, many new religions transformed their doctrines and became part of the Shinto system.

In 1899, the government issued the Regulations Concerning Propagation and Temples, Churches etc. of Religions Other Than Shinto and Buddhism. While indicating the government's recognition of the legality of Christianity, they in fact specifically intended to regulate Christianity in a similar way to Buddhism, including requiring the name and other details of the religion to be submitted to the local authority. As a result, virtually all religions in Japan were incorporated into the government's system.

Issues of Freedom of Religion and the Position of Shinto

Managing religions to promote nationalistic education and emperor worship, however, was inconsistent with the Meiji government's aim of building a state that would be internationally regarded as on par with advanced countries, including Western powers, in terms of freedom of religion and separation of state and religion. Facing increasing criticism from foreign governments, as well as from within the government and Buddhist schools, the government issued a notification in 1875 guaranteeing the freedom of religion. In 1877, it dissolved the Ministry of Religious Education.

This shift in religious policy naturally left the government with the question of how to promote nationalism, which had relied on emperor worship and hence the Shinto system. An obvious option that the government considered was to designate Shinto as Japan's official state religion while guaranteeing freedom of religion, following the examples of the United Kingdom and other countries, where both a state religion and freedom of religion existed. In fact, the government's influential bureaucrat and statesman Inoue Kowashi, in his "*Shūkyō no jiyū nitsuki ikensho*" [Opinion on freedom of religion] of 1884, referred to examples of the coexistence of a state religion and freedom of religion in several countries.[29] However, the government did not designate Shinto as the state religion, instead responding to the issue by arguing that Shinto was not a religion. In 1882, the government issued a notification to separate Shinto priests conducting imperial rituals from evangelists engaged in religious missionary work so as to identify the former as secular bureaucrats.

The government's stance of claiming the secularity of Shinto instead of designating it as the state religion represented its policy of promoting statolatry, using Shinto politically as its ideology instead of merely elevating its status. The government leveraged Shinto's actual religiosity, including the belief in the emperor's divinity, to render the state sacred. By placing supremacy on the emperor, and hence the state, without recognizing the transcendent values beyond them, as Murakami Shigeyoshi states, Shinto "exerted its function as the most effective political ideology for the state."[30] Thus, the secularity of Shinto as claimed by the government intended to avoid the actual unification of state and Shinto and thereby avoid criticism concerning freedom of religion and the separation of state and religion. While criticism was a factor in avoiding adoption of Shinto as a state religion, the Meiji regime was more focused on unifying the country. Hardacre's argument aligns with this view: "But the potential for conflict with the constitution was not the only reason. A deeper rationale lay in the determination to treat ideas about the Kami [or Shinto deity] as 'natural,' as are not appropriate for debate, something that all Japanese should agree upon and take for granted."[31]

Based on thus having granted Shinto a distinct status, the Meiji Constitution, promulgated in 1889 and officially named the Constitution of the Empire of Japan, explicitly indicated the government's stance of sacralizing the emperor and hence the state. Article 3 provided that "the Emperor is sacred and inviolable."[32] Although Article 28 referred to the freedom of religion, stating that "Japanese subjects shall, within limits not prejudicial to peace and order, and not antagonistic to their duties as subjects, enjoy freedom of religious belief,"[33] it granted that freedom only to the extent that it was consistent with the statolatry policy. The promulgation of the Constitution, in fact, completed the establishment of the ideological position of Shinto, which would later be referred to as State Shinto.[34]

The government used the school system to promote emperor worship, including requiring students to study and memorize the Imperial Rescript on Education, a document issued only a year after the promulgation of the Meiji Constitution and distributed to all schools in the country together with a portrait of the emperor. The Rescript emphasized Japan's unique *kokutai*, or national polity, which was considered to be based on a mystical bond between the divinized emperor and the country's people, referred to as *shinmin*, or the ruler's loyal subjects. It demanded from the people loyalty to the state and emperor, commanding that they "offer [themselves] courageously to the State" and "guard and maintain the prosperity of Our Imperial Throne coeval with heaven and earth."[35] In 1891, the Ministry of Education issued the Regulations for Elementary School Ceremonies on Festivals and Holidays that required schools to hold ceremonies on emperor-related holidays. These ceremonies entailed teachers and students bowing deeply in front of the portrait of the emperor and a copy of the Rescript, while the school principal read the Rescript aloud to the participants as they stood stiffly to attention. In the same year, Uchimura Kanzō, then a high school teacher, was forced to resign from the school following his refusal to bow deeply to the portrait of the emperor and a copy of the Rescript.[36]

While promoting State Shinto and emperor worship, the government sought to exclude other religions from school education. In 1899, the Ministry of Education issued an ordinance to distance general education from religion that prohibited not only public but also private schools from conducting religious education or ceremonies. Similar to the issue of the freedom of religion and the separation of state and religion, where State Shinto and emperor worship were treated as secular rituals, the government implemented the policy for separating education from religion solely to promote the worship of the emperor and, hence, state worship.

CONCLUSION

At the close of the nineteenth century, the Japanese state had managed to curtail those aspects of religion that appealed to universal or transcendent values. Religious energy was instead channeled into state leadership and the support of one government. In the early modern period prior to the Meiji Restoration, the country unifiers and Tokugawa government demolished resisting Buddhist groups; used more obedient, established schools of temple Buddhism as part of their state controlling system; and banned Christianity. Transcendent religiosity was virtually eliminated in Japan, which developed a secular civilizational backdrop against which the modern period commenced.

The West has, to some extent, achieved a balanced religion-state relationship through the interaction and competition between religion and state. Japan's path is perhaps the other way around. Historically, little to no transcendent religiosity or spiritual underpinnings have been established among the people, and hence no competition or balance between religion and state has occurred.

In the modern period, the Meiji government created State Shinto as an ideology for the worship of the emperor and hence the state, so as to quickly build a state that would be competitive in the international arena. Facing foreign pressure, the government sought to avoid the issue of freedom of religion by claiming the secularity of Shinto and incorporating a provision guaranteeing freedom of religion into its constitution. Eventually, however, the freedom of religion guaranteed by the constitution lost its substance, as State Shinto was elevated to the position of the de facto state religion while being officially recognized as secular. Other religions had to subordinate themselves to State Shinto or face persecution. Thus, in modern Japan, what was seemingly equivalent to the secularization of the state and of education was in actuality the process of promoting religious worship of the emperor and state while excluding other religions. The next chapter will show how Japan augmented the state control of religion in the early twentieth century by rejecting the religious transcendence that was adopted by the West and unifying the country under a single belief system.

NOTES

1. Kiri Paramore, "Premodern Secularism," *Japan Review* 30 (2017): 21–37.

2. Stephen Turnbull, *Japanese Warrior Monks AD 949–1603* (New York: Bloomsbury Publishing, 2012), 47–46.

3. Stephen Covell, *Japanese Temple Buddhism: Worldliness in a Religion of Renunciation* (Honolulu: University of Hawaii Press, 2005), 46–73.

4. Covell, *Japanese Temple Buddhism*, 46–73.

5. Satō Hiroo, *Nihon chūsei no kokka to bukkyō* [State and Buddhism in medieval Japan] (Tokyo: Yoshikawa Kobunkan, 2010), 249. All quotations from Satō are the author's translation unless stated otherwise.

6. Maruyama Masao, *Maruyama Masao kōgiroku* [The lectures of Maruyama Masao], Vol. 4 (Tokyo: University of Tokyo Press, 1998), 154. All quotations from Maruyama are the author's translation unless stated otherwise.

7. Maruyama, *Kōgiroku* [Lectures], Vol. 4, 155.

8. For example, the Taika Reform—a series of political reforms that followed the *coup d'état* of 645 led by Prince Nakano Ōe (later the emperor Tenji) against the Soga clan that had dominated the imperial court for half a century—saw Buddhism subordinated to the state authority based on *Sōni-ryō* (Regulations for Monks and Nuns) that allowed only regulated monks and nuns to conduct rituals while prohibiting them from promulgating their faith among people outside their temples.

9. Maruyama, *Kōgiroku* [Lectures], Vol. 4, 157.

10. Nichiren, "Shuju onfurumai gosho" [The actions of the votary of the Lotus Sutra], in *Nichiren Daishōnin Gosho Zenshū* [Collection of Literature of Nichiren], ed. Committee for Publishing the New Collection of Literature of Nichiren (Tokyo: Sōka Gakkai, 2021), 1227. All quotations from Nichiren are the author's translation unless stated otherwise.

11. Maruyama, *Kōgiroku* [Lectures], Vol. 4, 266.

12. Satō, *Kokka to bukkyō* [State and Buddhism], 244.

13. George Holmes, *The Oxford History of Medieval Europe* (Oxford and New York: Oxford University Press, 2001), 165–72.

14. Satō, *Kokka to bukkyō* [State and Buddhism], 249.

15. Tokugawa Government, "Shūmon Torishimari Kisoku" [Sect Control Regulations], in *Nihon shūkyō zenshi* [History of Japanese religions], Vol. 4, ed. Hiyane Antei (Tokyo: Kyobunkan 1942), 134.

16. Maruyama Masao, *Maruyama Masao kōgiroku* [The lectures of Maruyama Masao], Vol. 6 (Tokyo: University of Tokyo Press, 2000), 119–20.

17. Helen Hardacre, *Shinto: A History* (New York: Oxford University Press, 2017), 239.

18. Hardacre, *Shinto*, 239.

19. Tamamuro Fumio, *Edo bakufu no shūkyō tōsei* [Edo feudal government's religious control] (Tokyo: Hyoronsha, 1987), 62.

20. Satō Hiroo, *Kami, hotoke, ōken no chūsē* [Medieval Period of Gods, Buddhas, and Kingship] (Kyoto: Hozokan, 1998), 426.

21. Hardacre, *Shinto*, 423–65.

22. For detailed discussion of the history of the term "Shinto," refer to Kuroda Toshio, "Shinto in the History of Japanese Religion," trans. James Dobbins and Suzanne Gay, *Journal of Japanese Studies*, vol. 7, no. 1 (1981): 1–21.

23. John Breen and Mark Teeuwen, *A New History of Shinto* (Hoboken: John Wiley & Sons, 2010), 20.

24. Max Weber, *The Sociology of Religion*, trans. Ephraim Fischoff (Boston: Beacon Press, 1964), 25.

25. Kakubayashi Fumio, *Nihon kodai no seiji to keizai* [Politics and economy in Japan's ancient period] (Tokyo: Yoshikawa Kobunkan, 1998), 33–36.

26. There is much discussion about changes in the concept of religion in Japan and in translation of the term "religion," including eventually into *shūkyō*. See, for example, Hoshino Seiji, *Kindai Nihon no shūkyō gainen* [The concept of religion in modern Japan] (Tokyo: Yūshisha, 2012).

27. See the list of religion-related acts included in *Shūkyō to kokka* [Religion and state], ed. Yasumaru Yoshio and Miyachi Masato (Tokyo: Iwanami Shoten, 1988).

28. For a detailed discussion of the changes in Japanese Buddhist monks' stance on marriage, etc., see Minowa Kenryō, "Gendai Nihon bukkyo no tokuchō" [Characteristics of contemporary Japanese Buddhism], *Bulletin of the Faculty of Letters of Aichi Gakuin University* 38 (2008): 345–64.

29. Inoue Kowashi, "Shūkyō no jiyū nitsuki ikensho" [Opinion on freedom of religion], in *Nihon kindai shisō taikei* [A compendium of modern Japanese thoughts], Vol. 5, *Shūkyō to kokka* [Religion and state], ed. Yasumaru Yoshio and Miyachi Masato (Tokyo: Iwanami Shoten, 1988), 70–75.

30. Murakami Shigeyoshi, *Kokka Shinto* [State Shinto] (Tokyo: Iwanami Shoten, 1970), 119. All quotations from Murakami are the author's translation unless stated otherwise.

31. Hardacre, *Shinto*, 439.

32. Emperor of Meiji, *Dai-Nihon Teikoku Kenpō* [The Constitution of the Empire of Japan], promulgated February 11, 1889, trans. Itō Miyoji, https://www.ndl.go.jp/constitution/e/etc/c02.html (May 2, 2023).

33. Emperor of Meiji, *Teikoku Kenpō* [Constitution of the Empire].

34. The term "State Shinto" was introduced in the Shinto Directive, an order issued to the Japanese government in 1945 following the end of World War II by occupation authorities to abolish state support for Shinto. Some scholars prefer to describe this kind of Shinto as "state managed" or under "state management" though the distinction is more ideological than academic.

35. The English translation of the Rescript is based on the government's official translation, "The Imperial Rescript on Education—Translated into Chinese, English, French and German" (1909).

36. Hardacre, *Shinto*, 583.

Chapter 4

Modern Japan's Political Culture

Ultranationalism and Comparison of Ideas

As discussed in the previous chapter, Japanese civilization before the Meiji Restoration was characterized by the subordination of religious institutions to the secular authorities, and hence by the lack of "universal religiosity" in society. The term describes a religious appeal that transcends local secular interests. This religious vacuum gave the government of modern Japan the opportunity to create the artificial religion State Shinto and impose it on its entire population, forming a state-religion relationship unprecedented among modern nation-states. In fact, in Trent Maxey's words, "the very idea of religion, instead of being a pre-modern remnant that resisted secularization, emerged as a corollary to modernization and secular authority."[1] In this process, the authorities were able to gain control over the people through the stifling of religious sentiment that would transcend local or national secular interests. The need to establish a unified religion was a significant focus of the emperor during the first four decades of the twentieth century. The promotion of religion during this era was geared toward the creation of a ritual system to unify the nation in support of the imperial government. Religion was perceived as a powerful tool of influence that could affect the Japanese political system. During this period, the Shinto religion was used to promote the performance of state rituals.[2] The Shinto priesthood thrived under government patronage. It became more popular as it gained a more active role in government while also promoting the indigenous tradition in Japan.

This chapter will first examine the implications of modern Japan's religion-state relationship for the ultranationalism that drove the country to enter into World War II and to implement totalitarian control over its people. It will then seek to explain how the unification of government and State Shinto affected Japan's political culture by examining the text of *Kokutai no hongi* (The Cardinal Principles of the National Entity of Japan), a significant publication by the government in 1937 explicitly describing the militarist regime's ideology.[3] This chapter will also consider the philosophy of Makiguchi Tsunesaburō, a religious figure who died in prison during interrogation by the wartime prosecutor. There are a number of reasons for focusing on Makiguchi as part of the examination of relations between state and religion: first, comparing his thoughts to Japan's wartime ideology will help further highlight the weaknesses in the country's ultranationalism based on the unification of religion and government; second, Makiguchi's philosophy has been relatively little discussed in the academic space compared to better known Japanese thinkers of his time, such as Uchimura Kanzō and Fukuzawa Yukichi; and, third, the religious organization founded by Makiguchi has grown into one of the most influential religions in Japan after World War II, having considerable political impact by providing electoral endorsement to the country's recent ruling parties.

RELIGION IN PREWAR JAPAN

In the modern period leading up to the outbreak of Japan's bilateral regional wars with China and Russia and World War I and World War II, the imperial authorities had endeavored to establish control over religion such that the universal claims of Christianity and Buddhism could not affect political or social life. To that end, the Japanese government established a sanitized religion in the form of State Shinto to express totalitarian rule through militarism. Hence, religion in prewar Japan impacted the development of the nation by influencing several factors, ranging from economic aspects to political ones such as militarism. For instance, Japan's use of State Shinto as the leading "religion" made the regime increasingly militaristic. The government built many Shinto shrines enshrining late military commanders and generals throughout the country. Furthermore, the government in effect withdrew its stance claiming the secularism of State Shinto when it issued in 1932 a notification on the interpretation of the Ordinance to Distinguish General Education from Religions of 1899, which stated that "cultivating religious sentiment shall not be restrained at all."[4]

Additionally, the Wall Street crash or Black Thursday of 1929 and the subsequent Great Depression of the 1930s severely affected the Japanese economy, causing the country's export and domestic consumption to decline and its unemployment rate to rise. In response, the government, under Inukai Tsuyoshi's cabinet that came to power in 1931, took measures to repair the economy. These measures included abandoning the gold standard to let the Japanese yen depreciate, thereby enhancing the country's trade competitiveness and military expenditure to fuel domestic demand. Though these measures helped the Japanese economy to recover gradually, they also contributed to international tensions: the government policy to expand imports with the depreciated yen intensified economic competition with Western powers. Furthermore, the increase in military expenditure led to the rise of militarism, fueling the expanding power of the military.

RELIGION AND MILITARISM

The Meiji Constitution lacked a civilian-control mechanism over the military. With both "sacredness" and de facto sovereignty residing in the emperor, Article 11 of the Constitution, which reads "the Emperor has the supreme command of the Army and Navy,"[5] was interpreted as providing the military with autonomy from the civilian government. Prime Minister Inukai was assassinated by junior Navy and Army officers in May 1932 after struggling against the military's increasing influence, which marked an end to modern Japan's government having civilian prime ministers. After Saitō Makoto, a former admiral in the Navy, was appointed as the succeeding prime minister, the militarist regime took over and controlled the government until the end of World War II. In 1933, Japan left the League of Nations after its assembly issued a report condemning the country for its invasion and occupation of Manchuria, further isolating itself from the international community.

The rise of militarism supported by a religion-fueled ideology led to an increasingly intolerant government stance toward any religion that had doctrinal inconsistencies with State Shinto. The government extended the application of the legal instruments—*lèse-majesté* and the Maintenance of Public Order Law, which had originally been designed to control communists and later right-wing elements—to religions. In 1935, over five hundred police officers conducted a raid on the Kyoto headquarters of Ōmotokyō, a new religion, and its other branches throughout Japan, arresting over nine hundred leaders. This incident set a precedent for applying the Maintenance of Public Order Law to religious institutions. In the following year, the government set up religion-police units within every prefecture's Special Higher Police, the nationwide police network established and expanded during the 1910s and 1920s with the primary objective of rooting out communists. In 1937, the government charged another new religious institution called Hitonomichi Kyōdan with *lèse-majesté.*

Though the government dismantled these new religions, allegedly for their doctrinal deviation from State Shinto and hence for their aim of "changing the national polity," these charges were, as Sheldon Garon points out, "little more than legal pretexts."[6] If the government had truly targeted religions that deviated doctrinally from State Shinto, including questioning the divinity of the emperor, Garon wrote, "it would have started with the Christian denominations."[7] It would not have started with these new religions whose doctrines were basically, if not completely, in line with worship of the emperor. The root cause of the government's suppression of these new religions was their rapid growth and organizational autonomy. As Garon argues, "What ultimately sealed the fate of the new religions was not their teachings or rituals, but their rapid development outside the state-approved hierarchy of the established religions."[8]

Furthermore, Japan used Shinto to demonstrate its imperial control over its then colonies, without showing respect either to local people or to Japanese Shinto priests. For instance, when the colonial government of Taiwan constructed the imperial Major Grade shrine, the deities enshrined there were chosen by the colonial governor and did not include any native Taiwanese.[9] Similarly, the Japanese military governor of Korea turned down the Koreans' request for their national founder to be enshrined at the Korea Shrine, insisting that the Koreans should worship the Japanese imperial ancestors, despite Japanese Shinto priests' advocacy for the inclusion of local deities.[10] This case demonstrates that the military was the decision maker in religious affairs and that the Shinto priests lacked decisive weight in their views.

Militarist Japan's ideological use of State Shinto and intolerance of other religions was further strengthened under the cabinet of Hiranuma Kiichirō, who came to power in January 1939. The long-debated Religious Organizations Law was promulgated in April 1939 and enacted in the following year, aiming to strengthen governmental control of religion and requiring religious organizations to obtain approval from the government for their existence. Article 16 of the law allowed the government to withdraw its approval of any religious organizations that it deemed to be "prejudicial to peace and order, or antagonistic to their duties as subjects."[11] Furthermore, Article 5 provided that the withdrawal of approval would result in the dissolution of the relevant religious organization. Regarding the question of what would infringe the law by being "prejudicial to peace and order," Matsuo Chōzō, head of the Bureau of Religions at the Ministry of Education, the supervising authority for the operation of the Religious Organization Law, stated in front of the House of Peers: "If a religious organization or its teachers or equivalent refuse to visit and worship at Shinto shrines, or if they prevent someone from visiting and worshiping there, that would be obviously prejudicial to peace and order."[12] Thus, for religious organizations to obtain approval and to avoid dissolution, it was made compulsory to visit and worship at Shinto shrines as a way of ensuring these religions would perpetuate the practice of worshipping the emperor.

The reinforced relations between the militarist government and State Shinto were reflected in an increase in the number of Shinto shrines built in the Japanese colonies and foreign lands occupied by the Japanese, such as Taiwan, Korea, the South Sea Islands, and Singapore, with the total number of shrines exceeding sixteen hundred at their peak. For example, a shrine was built on the Korean Peninsula that enshrined three former emperors of ancient Japan who had led Japan's invasion of the peninsula. Korean school teachers who refused to worship at the Korea Shrine were dismissed. Christians in Korea were forced to worship at Shinto shrines "sometimes at the point of a bayonet."[13] Thus, State Shinto was used to control the people's thoughts by suppressing religions that were considered inconsistent with the official ideology and by sanctifying Japan's acts of aggression, both within Japan as well as in the lands it had seized or occupied.

Militarist Japan's State Shinto-based ideological control was further strengthened when the revised Maintenance of Public Order Law of 1941 was enacted several months before Japan's attack on Pearl Harbor. The waging of the Pacific War was beyond the country's military and economic capacity and necessitated totalitarian control of its people. One of the major changes made to the law was to criminalize religious leaders, and other group leaders, for "disavowing the national polity."[14] This was more broadly interpreted than the provision of the previous version of the law that prohibited organizations accused of "changing the polity."[15] Furthermore, the revised law explicitly enabled the authorities to punish leaders of groups for "impairing the sanctity and dignity of the shrines and Imperial Household."[16] The revised law's main target groups were obviously religious organizations that indicated any inconsistency with State Shinto. Though not explicitly, the militarist government thus revealed the religious nature of State Shinto, the preceding administrations having denied it since the beginning of the Meiji period. This shift in stance illustrates that continuing to fight the controversial war necessitated a religion-fueled ideology to support the illusionary concept of a "holy war" for Japan as a "divine" land. As Murakami Shigeyoshi puts it, Shinto shrines were vested with "a new religious function of praying for winning the war."[17]

Under the revised Maintenance of Public Order Law, many religious denominations suffered persecution. Among Christian denominations, over a hundred followers of the Japanese Holiness Church were arrested after Koyama Sōsuke, pastor of the church in Hokkaido, was himself arrested for refusing to visit and worship at Shinto shrines. He later died while under interrogation at the region's police detention facility. The Buddhist lay group Sōka Gakkai, then called Sōka Kyōiku Gakkai, was suppressed for its refusal to worship talismans from Ise Grand Shrine. Sōka Gakkai's leaders were arrested, and its president, Makiguchi Tsunesaburō, died while under interrogation at Tokyo Detention Center.

On the other hand, most religious organizations, including more established Buddhist schools and Christian churches, adjusted "to the new doctrinal absolutism and thus escaped direct persecution."[18] For example, the Nichiren Shōshū Buddhist sect, with which Sōka Gakkai was affiliated as its lay organization, not only accepted the worship of

Shinto talismans but denied its affiliation with Sōka Gakkai, including prohibiting Makiguchi from visiting its head temple after Makiguchi refused to accept an instruction from the sect's high priest, Suzuki Nikkyō, to worship talismans.[19] Furthermore, high priest Suzuki issued a written notification to the sect's priests, instructing them to encourage their lay believers to worship at Ise Grand Shrine.[20] In fact, the contrast between Nichiren Shōshū and Sōka Gakkai exemplifies why certain religious bodies escaped persecution and others suffered persecution, despite having common doctrinal underpinnings. The militarist government rewarded Nichiren Shōshū for its obedience by approving it as a religious organization under the Religious Organizations Law in May 1943, or ten months after Makiguchi's arrest and eighteen months before his death. This shows that the government of Japan was focused only on whether a religion was compliant with worshipping the state and the emperor; it had less concern about the doctrine itself. Moreover, the militaristic government that advocated a universal Shinto state showed great partiality in terms of the measures taken against other religious sects based on that sect's compliance with the governing rules. In fact, leaders of the deviant sects would suffer persecution under the militaristic government, while obedient religious sects would be rewarded with government approval.

Modern Japan's extreme nationalism, associated with militarism and internal thought control, is often referred to as ultranationalism. Although, as Maruyama states, "a tendency to military expansion was an inherent impulse in nationalism" among many European countries in the age of imperialism,[21] modern Japan's political culture became extraordinarily fanatical, as demonstrated by the kamikaze attacks. It is quite true that nationalism in Japan was guided by this impulse to a stronger degree and that it manifested in a clearer way than in other countries. However, this is not merely a matter of quantity. Maruyama points out a qualitative difference between other countries' nationalism and Japan's ultranationalism. Quite apart from any difference in degree, there is a difference in the inner motivating power that spurred Japan to expansion abroad and to oppression at home, and it is only because of this qualitative difference that Japanese nationalism acquired its "ultra" aspect.[22]

This qualitative shift was explicitly demonstrated when the Ministry of Education published a work of indoctrination, the Cardinal Principles.

This document, which will be discussed in more detail later in this chapter, promoted "Japan's supposed mission to rule the world."[23] Maruyama finds the key to this qualitative difference in the concept of state neutrality regarding religious and other internal values.

> A comparison with European nationalism will lead us to the crux of the matter. As Carl Schmidt has pointed out, an outstanding characteristic of the modern European State lies in its being *ein neutraler Staat.* That is to say, the State adopts a neutral position on internal values, such as the problem of what truth and justice are; it leaves the choice and judgement of all values of this sort to special groups (for instance, to the Church) or to the conscience of the individual.[24]

Modern Japan, however, did not achieve the religious neutrality of the state. In Maruyama's words, "Japanese nationalism strove consistently to base its control on internal values rather than authority deriving from external laws."[25] Further, unlike in the case of European nationalism, "in Japan there was no ecclesiastical force to assert the supremacy of any 'internal' world" over the combined secular and religious authority of the state.[26] As a result, "Japanese morality never underwent the process of interiorization that we have seen in the case of the West," and the state was considered the "ultimate source of both ethics and power."[27]

The consequent "automatic righteousness" therefore justified the "most atrocious behaviour, the most treacherous acts" of the country, both externally and internally.[28] Externally, for example, kamikaze attacks were used toward the end of World War II when Japan's defeat was becoming increasingly assured. Far from being rational, the militarist government enforced these actions based on the logic that the righteous cause triumphs. Domestically, any religion that the government considered to be questioning this righteousness became subject to persecution, as discussed in the preceding chapter. State Shinto, the effectively artificial religion created by the government, was, therefore, the ideology for endorsing the state's righteousness.

REVIEW OF *KOKUTAI NO HONGI* (THE CARDINAL PRINCIPLES OF THE NATIONAL STRUCTURE)

Kokutai no hongi (The Cardinal Principles of the National Structure) was issued as an official publication by the Meiji government in 1937 and circulated in millions of copies during the period when the government was increasingly tightening control, including implementing full-scale clampdowns on many religious groups. The team that authored this text included Kōno Seizō and Miyaji Naokazu, who acted as the main contributors.[29] The major objective of the text in regard to religion was to establish a state of universality. It discouraged the formation of many religious groups, therefore advocating a common mode of worship with the end goal of ensuring universal loyalty to a single emperor and a common state. In this way, the autocratic government of Japan wanted to establish a more efficient strategy of controlling its people through a common Shinto religion.

The document was later edited mainly by Itō Enkichi, chief of the Bureau of Thought Control and later vice-minister of education. The Cardinal Principles was essentially militarist Japan's major ideological textbook. Robert Kind Hall, editor of the English translation of the Cardinal Principles published after World War II, began translation work before serving as chief of the Education Sub-Section of the Civil Information and Education Section, General Headquarters, Supreme Commander for the Allied Powers. He wrote in the editor's introduction to the English book: "The importance of the *Kokutai no Hongi* as a political and educational policy document was then fully recognized, and a rough translation was begun under [the editor's] direction."[30] The prefatory note to the English publication starts with the following paragraph:

> On December 15, 1945, General Douglas MacArthur, Supreme Commander for the Allied Powers in Tokyo, forwarded to the Imperial Japanese Government his historic Shinto Directives, AG000.3 (15 Dec 45) CIE. Its formal title was "Abolition of Governmental Sponsorship, Support, Perpetuation, Control, and Dissemination of State Shinto." It was more than an attempt to separate church and state. It was a direct attack on the very essence of the official national philosophy. Paragraph *1h* of this directive specifically forbade the governmental circulation

> of the *Kokutai no Hongi* (Cardinal Principles of the National Entity of Japan).[31]

Roy Miller describes the significance of the Cardinal Principles, stating, "It contained the official teaching of the Japanese state on every aspect of domestic policy, international affairs, culture, and civilization."[32] In fact, reviewing the content of the Cardinal Principles reveals the essential ideological underpinnings of modern Japan's political culture, including the unity of State Shinto and government, rejection of the rule of law and democracy, and the denial of universality, human rights, and individualism. Referring to the Cardinal Principles as one of the "ideological screeds" of the time, Hardacre describes the document as fanatical because it entails a great deal of self-sacrifice by featuring "passionate adulation of death in war."[33] It is obvious, as John Brownlee points out, that the government was "no longer dealing . . . with a political theory of Japan designed to accommodate modern institutions of government, like the Meiji Constitution."[34] Universality was a major focus that implied universal membership in the respective parishes.[35] In this case, everyone living within the premises of a shrine was obliged to support it in all circumstances. All the endeavors of the militaristic government were geared toward the establishment of a universal religion to attain ultimate control over the people's beliefs. However, the religious leaders of Shintoism lacked authoritative power in matters pertaining to the government or even the practice of the religion itself. The government had substantial control and influence over the shrines, to the extent that it determined the religious deities for Shinto.

Unification of State and State Shinto

The Cardinal Principles claim the divinity of the emperor and hence the sacredness of state affairs as governed by the living god.

> The government of our country is administered by the Emperor, who . . . as deity incarnate leads his people. . . . Hence, the government of our country is a sacred undertaking and by no means a private affair.[36]

In this context, the government of Japan was perceived to be sacred to the extent that its people worshipped the emperor, who was treated like a god based on the belief that a deity was incarnated in him to lead a holy state. This concept was a key ideology under which the universality of religion in Japan was to be attained, because it meant that Shintoism would be upheld while suppressing other religions that defied the rules and regulations of the government and the Imperial Constitution. The Cardinal Principles argue that the emperor is different from other rulers in the context of the Imperial Constitution, which defines the Emperor as "sacred and inviolate," stating:

> The Emperor differs from the sovereigns of foreign countries, is not a ruler set up by reason of necessity for the administration of a country, nor is he a sovereign chosen and settled upon by the subjects on the ground of intelligence or virtues.
>
> The Emperor is an august descendant of Amaterasu Ohmikami (Sun Goddess) and is a divine offspring of the Imperial Ancestors.[37]

This article was meant to echo the essence of the emperor figure, whose throne was considered sacred. Unlike other government structures whose leaders may be chosen out of necessity, the position of the emperor was regarded as divine through the incarnation of the imperial ancestors.

Moreover, the Cardinal Principles explicitly declare the unification of government and State Shinto, including the last section of the pamphlet, starting with a subsection on Unity of Religious Rites and the State.

> The Emperor becomes one in essence with the Imperial Ancestors through the religious rites. . . . Therefore, the conducting of the religious rites and the work of administration are in their principle united.[38]
>
> In our country, religious rites and the administration spring from the same source under the august rule of the Emperors who succeeded each other in an unbroken line.[39]

At the same time, the Cardinal Principles sought to justify Japan's aggression by referring to it as an expression of the emperor's "love for the people" and describing the emperor's enshrining of the war dead at Yasukuni Shrine as his "august compassion."

> The Sino-Japanese and Russo-Japanese Wars, the annexation of Korea, and the efforts exerted in the founding of Manchukuo, are one and all but expressions of the great august Will replying to the august benevolence seen in the granting of the Land by the Imperial Ancestor to the

Grandchild, on the one hand, and on the other the promoting of the peace of the country and the advancement of the great task of love for the people, thus radiating the grace of the Imperial Throne.[40]

. . . we respectfully witness the Emperor's august compassion, which exceeds a parent's love for his child. The Emperor's deeds that remain with us are so many as to defy enumeration when we cite such things as how he enshrines as deities in Yasukuni Shrine those loyal subjects that have sacrificed their lives for the nation.[41]

Furthermore, the Cardinal Principles apply the idea of the oneness of State Shinto and government to the Imperial Military Forces and thereby seek to hallow the warriors.

The manifestation of our national entity is just the same, also in the case of our military affairs. Since ancient times the spirits of the deities in our country have fallen into two groups: the spirits of peace and the spirits of warriors. . . . It is in the subduing of those who refuse to conform to the august influence of the Emperor's virtues that the mission of our Imperial Military Forces lies, and thus we see the Way of the warriors that may be called Jimmu [Divine Warrior].[42]

Thus, the Cardinal Principles stressed the sacredness of the emperor, the state, and the military and sought to justify Japan's acts of war. They demonstrated the position of State Shinto as the religiously reinforced ideology of the militarist government.

Rejection of Democracy and Rule of Law

The second characteristic of the Cardinal Principles was the rejection of democracy and the rule of law. The Cardinal Principles refer to the Meiji Constitution as an imperial decree, differentiating it from constitutions established as fundamental legal norms in other countries, denying constitutionalism and the rule of law, and thereby justifying autocracy under the name of the emperor.

The written Constitutions of foreign countries have come into existence as a result, in the main, of expelling or suppressing the existing order. In the case of a Constitution resulting from the expulsion of a ruler, the thing is called a Constitution Based on Social Contract. . . . However, our Imperial Constitution is a Constitution Granted by the Throne.[43]

The imperial constitution was thus based on the belief that the throne was divine and the emperor was an incarnation of the ancestors. In this case, democracy was not embraced, as the will of the emperor was directly imposed on the people. This is contrary to other constitutions in which democracy ensures that no one is above the rule of law.

> The Emperor is the holder in essence of supreme power; so that the theory which holds the view that sovereignty lies in essence in the State and that the Emperor is but its organ has no foundation except for the fact that it is a result of blindly following the theories of Western States.[44]

The emperor was perceived to possess power over the Constitution in which he defines rules to be followed. Therefore, the state rejected the rule of law. In fact, described as *tenno no shinsei*, or direct rule by the emperor, autocracy is bluntly admitted in the Cardinal Principles.

> Above all, the basic principles underlying the form of government are not those seen in the entrusting of administration to the throne in and following the Middle Ages [*chūsei*], nor those of the British type of government in which "the sovereign reigns but does not rule"; nor yet are they the principles underlying joint government by a sovereign and his subjects; no more are they those underlying the policy of mutual independence of the legislature or the policy of binding everything under the law, but are entirely the basic principles of direct rule by the Emperor.[45]

The Cardinal Principles further emphasize autocracy by denying the separation of powers as a checks-and-balances system.

> The triune subsistence, for example, of the Government, courts of justice, and the Diet, is different from the mutual independence of the legislature as it exists among Western nations, which aims at depriving the one holding sovereign power of judicial and legislative powers, giving recognition only to, yet at the time of curbing, his administrative power, with a view to restraining the powers of the ruler; for in our country segregation is not in respect of the rights of a ruler, but applies merely to the organs for the assistance of the direct Imperial rule, whose object is to make ever more secure the assistance extended to the direct rule by the Emperor. The deliberative assembly, too, is in a so-called democratic country, a representative organ of a people who are normal rulers; . . . Our Imperial Diet, on the other hand, is completely different, since it was instituted

> with the one object of providing the people with a means of assisting the Emperor's direct rule in special ways in regard to special matters.[46]

Therefore, the Cardinal Principles reveal the autocratic nature of the government of the time, explicitly rejecting democracy and the rule of law. The document was distributed to schoolteachers so that, in Hardacre's words, they could "counter 'dangerous thought' among the young."[47] The teachers were thus used as the vessels to transmit the statist ideas to their students.

Denial of Human Rights, Individualism, and Other Basic Ethical Values and Ideas

Another characteristic of the Cardinal Principles, correlating with the denial of democracy and the rule of law, is the denial of human rights, individualism, and other universal and transcendent values and ideas, while emphasizing particular national values and demanding subordination and loyalty from the people. Under the section on *Shinmin* or the Way of Subjects, the Cardinal Principles differentiate Japan's "subjects" from "citizens" in Western countries, denying individualism and enforcing loyalty to the emperor and state.

> We subjects are intrinsically quite different from the so-called citizens of Occidental countries. The relationship between ruler and subject is not of a kind in which the people are correlated to the sovereign or in which there is first a people for whose prosperity and well-being a rule is established.[48]
>
> We must sweep aside the corruption of the spirit and the clouding of knowledge that arises from setting up one's "self" and from being taken up with one's "self" and return to a pure and clear state of mind that belongs intrinsically to us as subjects, and thereby fathom the great principle of loyalty.[49]

The Cardinal Principles deny the inherent rights of individuals and instead define the rights of subjects only as privileges extended by the emperor. In this sense, the rights of the people are tailored to support the ruler without any protection against the personal interest of the ruler. Human rights are perceived as the emperor's provision of care to his subjects.

All laws in the Imperial Constitutions on the form of government are but extensions and transmissions of this principle of direct Imperial rule. For instance, stipulations on the rights and duties of Sovereign and subject are different from those which exist among Western nations where a system of free rights serves to protect the inherent rights of the people from the ruler, for the stipulations are the fruit of the Emperor's fond care for his people and his great august spirit to provide them with equal opportunities for assisting the Throne without feelings of barrier.[50]

Obviously, in such a system, there is no room for universal religious appeal. All religious enthusiasm is rechanneled to adoration of the emperor. The Cardinal Principles further deny individual rights to freedom, equality, and independence.

The basic characteristics of modern Occidental cultures lie in the fact that an individual is looked upon as an existence of an absolutely independent being, all cultures comprising the perfection of this individual being who in turn is the creator and determiner of all values. . . . The greater part of Occidental theories of State and political concepts so evolved do not view the State as being a nuclear existence that gives birth to individual beings, which it transcends, but as an expedient for the benefit, protection, and enhancement of the welfare of individual persons; so that these theories have become expressions of the principles of subsistence which have at their center free, equal, and independent individuals.[51]

On the other hand, the Cardinal Principles demand of the people selfless loyalty to the emperor and state: they are expected to devote their total obedience and service in support of the emperor. Hence, each person is treated as an asset of the state with the utmost reverence of the emperor.

Loyalty means to reverence the Emperor as [our] pivot and to follow him implicitly. By implicit obedience is meant casting ourselves aside and serving the Emperor intently. To walk this Way of loyalty is the sole Way in which we subjects "live," and the fountainhead of all energy. Hence, offering our lives for the sake of the Emperor does not mean so-called self-sacrifice, but the casting aside of our little selves to live under his august grace and the enhancing of the genuine life of the people of a State. . . . The ideology which interprets the relationship between the Emperor and his subjects as being a reciprocal relationship such as merely [involves] obedience to authority or rights and duties, rests on individualistic ideologies and is a rationalistic way of thinking that looks

> on everything as being in equal personal relationships. An individual is an existence belonging to a State and her history, which forms the basis of his origin, and is fundamentally one body with it.[52]

Thus, the Cardinal Principles deny individuals their universal and transcendent human rights, freedom, and independence, and instead demand their subordination and loyalty to the emperor and the state.

In particular, the Cardinal Principles strongly emphasize particular national values and ideas. For example, a concluding sentence of the section on National Culture reads: "In a word, our culture is, in its essence, a manifestation of the great spirit of the founding of the Empire, and scholastic pursuits, education, artistic pursuits, etc., all spring from one and the same source."[53]

Also, referring to Buddhism, the Cardinal Principles deny its transcendent aspects and only accept a statist version.

> Buddhism in India has acetic and intuitive aspects, but as it is a product of imaginative and unrealistic racial traits, it is meditative, unhistorical, and transcends the State. However, in its assimilation by our nation, it was sublimated and fused into our national spirit, contributing much toward enriching the fountainhead of the State.[54]

This description of Buddhism as a religion having been fused into wartime Japan's national spirit reflects the fact that, by the time of the publication of the document, the overwhelming majority of Buddhist denominations in their effort to escape persecution had "adjusted to the new doctrinal absolutism."[55] In these ways, the Cardinal Principles fueled and made sacred the unchecked power of the emperor and hence of the militarist government. Underlying the Cardinal Principles was modern Japan's ideology that emphasized particularism and denied universal and transcendent values and ideas, including democracy, the rule of law, and human rights. State Shinto played a central role in formulating and disseminating this ideology.

MAKIGUCHI TSUNESABURŌ AND HIS RELIGIOUS AND POLITICAL PERSPECTIVES

Makiguchi Tsunesaburō was a reformist educator who founded Sōka Kyōiku Gakkai (the Society for Value-Creating Education), predecessor to the lay Nichiren Buddhist body Sōka Gakkai. He was born in Japan's Niigata Prefecture in 1871, three years after the Meiji government came into power, and he lived until 1944. As described in the preceding chapter, he died in prison following his arrest by the militarist government as part of its persecution of disobedient religious groups. Nakazawa Shunsuke refers to Makiguchi as an example of the few religious figures who "maintained their faiths during these incidents while there were those people who quickly indicated their apostasy."[56] This section will explore Makiguchi's ideas in a broader context, studying their contrast with modern Japan's ideology in terms of both religious ideas and political ideas pertaining to religion and examining why the militarist government considered them subversive.

Makiguchi embraced Nichiren Buddhism in 1928. As described in the preceding chapter, the political scientist Maruyama highlighted the Buddhist concept often cited by Nichiren, "Rely on the dharma, and not on the person." This concept attracted Makiguchi, too, who wrote:

> The tenet "rely on the dharma, and not on the person" is also consistent with the principle of constitutional government that civilized countries embrace alike in the twentieth century. In this case, the expected or inherent nature greatly depends on the constitution which defines the rules and regulations that should be followed by the government. In the context of religion, the constitutional government could have some influence on the activities of a given religious sect, hence determining the nature of the nation in regard to religious matters.[57]

For Makiguchi, the concept of "rely on the dharma, and not on the person" served as a religious foundation for his emphasis on constitutionalism and the rule of law. Thus, Makiguchi's emphasis on the rule of law had religious and philosophical underpinnings. Meanwhile, by emphasizing the intellect, Makiguchi combined secular thinking with his religious beliefs. Shimazono Susumu states:

> Although Makiguchi Tsunesaburō followed the exclusive belief system of Nichiren Shōshū,[58] if he had not smartly incorporated the pragmatic pedagogical and sociological thoughts that he had previously learned, the Sōka Gakkai would not have seen its development.[59]

Takeuchi Keiichi presents a similar view, stating that Makiguchi "did not, under any circumstances, abandon the rational way of thinking that the modern sciences involved" and emphasizing that his rejection of State Shinto was based on both his religious belief and "his acceptance of the rational logic of modern science."[60] Makiguchi did not find any major conflict between reason and religious beliefs and considered both religion and rational thinking, making his political decisions religiously informed. Although he believed in the Nichiren Shōshū religion, his rational thinking—or the knowledge he had acquired through modern science backed up by his religious beliefs—contributed to his independent stance and refusal to accept State Shinto.

Makiguchi's political thoughts were particularly inclined toward a religious perspective and human rights, as seen in his consistent writings emphasizing the rule of law, including his major works, *Jinsei chirigaku* (Human Geography) and *Sōka kyōikugaku taikei* (The System of Value-Creating Education). In *Human Geography*, this is reflected in his reference to various classifications of country, where Makiguchi pays particular attention to the distinction between constitutional and nonconstitutional countries, stating, "If classification is needed to indicate the cultural levels of nations, the distinction between constitutional and non-constitutional countries is considered rather appropriate."[61] Furthermore, in the System for Value-Creating Pedagogy, which was published in 1931 when Japan was becoming increasingly militaristic, Makiguchi explicitly emphasizes constitutionalism and the rule of law.

> Every country in its age of autocracy was governed by person(s) rather than by law. However, as the general public gradually became knowledgeable, the law came to be considered more significant than the person(s). Essential to today's constitutional government is the pledge, where once a constitution is established, even the sovereign must respect and not breach it.[62]

Makiguchi's emphasis on constitutionalism and the rule of law is in contrast to the ideas expressed in the aforementioned government publication, Cardinal Principles, where the Meiji Constitution is referred to only as a decree endorsing the emperor's autocratic ruling. Rather than supporting the rights of the people, the Meiji Constitution fostered imperial rule with more focus on the emperor being above the rule of law, and the people being required to worship State Shinto and the emperor. During this era, religious freedom violations were rampant because subjects were denied the right to practice their own religions and forced toward universal observance of Shinto.

Furthermore, in his description of the role of states, Makiguchi stresses the state's function to protect individual rights.

> Part of the state's functions clearly recognized among civilized countries is not only to recognize individual rights against infringement by the government, the organ of state power itself, and to make individual freedom sacred and inviolable and guarantee political rights (suffrage) for individuals, but also to provide methods for exercising and enforcing their rights.[63]

In this regard, too, Makiguchi's ideas contrast with the militarist government's ideology, which denies the inherent rights of individuals, instead defining the rights of "subjects" only as privileges extended by the emperor, as expressed in the Cardinal Principles. Makiguchi's emphasis on the sacredness and inviolability of individual rights is also in direct contrast to the Meiji Constitution, which in Article 3 stipulates that "the Emperor is sacred and inviolable."[64]

Makiguchi was arrested by the thought police, the Special Higher Police, in 1943 for an alleged breach of the Maintenance of Public Order Law and lèse-majesté. During interrogation, among many other statements that bluntly rejected State Shinto, Makiguchi referred to the emperor as an "ordinary human being" who is "not free from making mistakes."[65] He thus denied the emperor's divinity, the core of State Shinto, directly confronting the militarist government's ideology. In his view, it was wrong to perceive the emperor as a flawless being. However, the government considered his position treasonous, leading to Makiguchi's imprisonment. Makiguchi maintained his standpoint until he died in prison at the age of seventy-three.

CONCLUSION

Modern Japan's ultranationalist fueling of military expansion and the use of totalitarian thought-control was based on State Shinto fanaticism. Shinto was used by the state as a tactic to unify the nation to obtain totality in ruling. Therefore, as a means of uniting the country, religion was incorporated into the government structure to ensure that people worshipped the emperor and the state. The militarist authorities' ideology, as expressed in the Cardinal Principles, openly promoted the unity of State Shinto and government and rejected democracy, the rule of law, human rights, individualism, and other transcendent values.

This chapter's discussion has also referred to Makiguchi, whose political, educational, and religious ideas contrasted sharply with the militarist authorities' ideology. Makiguchi championed the rule of law, human rights, and individual intellectual creativity while denying the divinity of the emperor and the foundation of State Shinto in his writings and during interrogation by the thought police. The decision by the government to arrest Makiguchi and keep him in prison until his death illustrates how the values and positions he upheld were considered a threat to the state, considering the authorities' dependence on totalitarian spiritual control of the people rooted in the State Shinto system.

NOTES

1. Trent Maxey, *The "Greatest Problem": Religion and State Formation in Meiji Japan* (Cambridge: Harvard University Press, 2014), 242.
2. Maxey, *Greatest Problem*, 100.
3. As mentioned in the notes of the introduction of this book, there are a variety of English translations of the title *Kokutai no hongi*. Unless stated otherwise, the English translation used in this book follows the title of the official English version of *Kokutai no hongi*, *Cardinal Principles of the National Entity of Japan*, edited by Robert Hall and published by Harvard University Press in 1949, which is also included in the bibliography.
4. Ministry of Education, *"Ippan no kyōiku wo shūkyō igai ni tokuritsu sesimuru kunrei no kaishaku ni kansuru ken"* [Notification on the interpretation of the ordinance to distinguish general education from religions], Bureau of Religions and Bureau of General Educational Affairs Notification No. 102, in *Meiji igo shūkyō kankei hōrei ruisan* [Collection of religion-related laws and ordinances since the Meiji era], ed. Ministry of Education (Tokyo: Daiichihoki

Shuppan, 1968), 948. The quotation is the author's translation of this part of the Ministry of Education's notification.

5. Emperor of Meiji, *Dai-Nihon Teikoku Kenpō* [The Constitution of the Empire of Japan], promulgated February 11, 1889, trans. Ito Miyoji, https://www.ndl.go.jp/constitution/e/etc/c02.html (May 2, 2023).

6. Sheldon Garon, *Molding Japanese Minds: The State in Everyday Life* (Princeton: Princeton University Press, 1997), 81.

7. Garon, *Molding Japanese Minds*, 81.

8. Garon, *Molding Japanese Minds*, 83.

9. Helen Hardacre, *Shinto: A History* (New York: Oxford University Press, 2017), 406.

10. Hardacre, *Shinto*, 432.

11. Imperial Diet, *Shūkyō Dantai Hō* [Religious Organizations Law], promulgated April 8, 1939, https://www.digital.archives.go.jp/img/137999 (April 26, 2023). All quotations from the provisions of the Religious Organizations Law are the author's translations unless stated otherwise.

12. House of Peers, *Dai 74-kai Teikoku Gikai Kizokuin Shūkyō Dantaihōan Tokubetsu Iinkai gijiroku dai ichi gō* [The minutes of the meeting of Special Committee on Religious Organizations Bill, House of Peers, the 74th Session of the Imperial Diet, No. 1], January 25, 1939, https://teikokugikai-i.ndl.go.jp/minutes/api/emp/v1/detailPDF/img/007401484X00119390125 (April 24, 2023). The quotation is the author's translation.

13. Hardacre, *Shinto*, 433.

14. Imperial Diet, *Chian Iji Hō Kaisei Hō* [Act to Revise the Maintenance of Public Order Law], promulgated March 8, 1941, https://www.digital.archives.go.jp/img/147953 (April 24, 2023). All quotations from the provisions of the Act to Revise the Maintenance of Public Order Law are the author's translations unless stated otherwise.

15. Imperial Diet, *Chian Iji Hō* [Maintenance of Public Order Law], promulgated April 22, 1925, https://www.digital.archives.go.jp/img/1643344 (April 24, 2023). All quotations from the provisions of the Maintenance of Public Order Law are the author's translations unless stated otherwise.

16. Imperial Diet, *Chian Iji Hō Kaisei Hō* [Act to Revise the Maintenance of Public Order Law].

17. Murakami Shigeyoshi, *Kokka Shinto* [State Shinto] (Tokyo: Iwanami Shoten, 1970), 144.

18. Garon, *Molding Japanese Minds*, 85.

19. Refer, for example, to the Committee for Compiling Chronological Records of Makiguchi Tsunesaburō and Toda Jōsei, eds., *Nenpu Makiguchi Tsunesaburō Toda Jōsei* [Chronological records of Makiguchi Tsunesaburō and Toda Jōsei] (Tokyo: Daisanbunmeisha, 1993).

20. Nichiren Shōshū Head Temple, *Nichiren Shōshū intatsu* [Nichiren Shōshū official notification], no. 2328, October 10, 1942, cited in Nichiren Shōshū's official bulletin *Dai-Nichiren* (November 1942), 1.

21. Maruyama Masao, *Thought and Behavior in Modern Japanese Politics* (London: Oxford University Press, 1969), 2. Quotations from Maruyama's *Thought and Behaviors in Modern Japanese Politics* are cited from the English-translated version of the book; they are, therefore, not the author's translations as are the case with other quotations from his work.

22. Maruyama, *Thought and Behavior*, 2–3.

23. Hardacre, *Shinto*, 434.

24. Maruyama, *Thought and Behavior*, 3.

25. Maruyama, *Thought and Behavior*, 4.

26. Maruyama, *Thought and Behavior*, 4.

27. Maruyama, *Thought and Behavior*, 9.

28. Maruyama, *Thought and Behavior*, 9.

29. Hardacre, *Shinto*, 434.

30. Rober Hall, ed., *Kokutai No Hongi: Cardinal Principles of the National Entity of Japan*, trans. John Gauntlett (Cambridge: Harvard University Press, 1949), 3.

31. Hall, *Cardinal Principles*, v.

32. Roy Andrew Miller, *Japan's Modern Myth* (New York: Weatherhill, 1982), 92.

33. Hardacre, *Shinto*, 434–35.

34. John S. Brownlee, "Four Stages of the Japanese Kokutai (National Essence)," paper presented at the Japan Studies Association of Canada Conference, Kelowna, British Columbia, October 2000, 10, https://www.adilegian.com/PDF/brownlee.pdf (May 13, 2023).

35. Hardacre, *Shinto*, 376.

36. Ministry of Education, *Kokutai no hongi* [Cardinal principles of the national entity of Japan], March 30, 1937. The quotation is from the government publication's English translation *Kokutai No Hongi: Cardinal Principles of the National Entity of Japan*, ed. Robert Hall, trans. John Gauntlett (Cambridge: Harvard University Press, 1949), 64.

37. Ministry of Education, *Hongi* [Cardinal principles], 71.

38. Ministry of Education, *Hongi* [Cardinal principles], 73.

39. Ministry of Education, *Hongi* [Cardinal principles], 160.

40. Ministry of Education, *Hongi* [Cardinal principles], 75.

41. Ministry of Education, *Hongi* [Cardinal principles], 77.

42. Ministry of Education, *Hongi* [Cardinal principles], 170.

43. Ministry of Education, *Hongi* [Cardinal principles], 161.

44. Ministry of Education, *Hongi* [Cardinal principles], 165.

45. Ministry of Education, *Hongi* [Cardinal principles], 165.

46. Ministry of Education, *Hongi* [Cardinal principles], 166.
47. Hardacre, *Shinto*, 434.
48. Ministry of Education, *Hongi* [Cardinal principles], 79.
49. Ministry of Education, *Hongi* [Cardinal principles], 82.
50. Ministry of Education, *Hongi* [Cardinal principles], 166.
51. Ministry of Education, *Hongi* [Cardinal principles], 180.
52. Ministry of Education, *Hongi* [Cardinal principles], 80–81.
53. Ministry of Education, *Hongi* [Cardinal principles], 159.
54. Ministry of Education, *Hongi* [Cardinal principles], 178.
55. Garon, *Molding Japanese Minds*, 85.
56. Nakazawa Shunsuke, *Chian Ijihō* [The Maintenance of Public Order Law] (Tokyo: Chuokoron-shinsha, 2012), 191. All quotations from Nakazawa are the author's translations unless stated otherwise.
57. Makiguchi Tsunesaburō, *Sōka kyōikugaku taikei* [The system of value-creating education], vol. 2 (Tokyo: Fuzanbo, 1931), 197. All quotations from Makiguchi are the author's translations unless stated otherwise.
58. Nichiren Shōshū is a branch of the Nichiren school of Buddhism.
59. Shimazono Susumu, *Gendai kyūsai shūkyō-ron* [A study of modern salvation religion] (Tokyo: Seikyusha, 1992), 75. All quotations from Shimazono are the author's translations unless stated otherwise.
60. Takeuchi Keiichi, *Modern Japanese Geography: An Intellectual History* [In Japanese] (Tokyo: Kokon Shoin, 2000), 120.
61. Makiguchi Tsunesaburō, *Jinsei chirigaku* [Human geography], eighth edition (Tokyo: Bunkaido Shoten, 1908), 899.
62. Makiguchi, *Sōka kyōikugaku* [Value-creating education], Vol. 2, 197–98.
63. Makiguchi Tsunesaburō, *Jinsei chirigaku* [Human geography], first edition (Tokyo: Bunkaido Shoten, 1903), 869.
64. Emperor of Meiji, *Dai-Nihon Teikoku Kenpō* [The Constitution of the Empire of Japan].
65. Home Ministry, "Sōka Kyōiku Gakkai kaichō Makiguchi Tsunesaburō ni taisuru jinmon chōsho bassui" [Excerpts from the records of interrogation of Makiguchi Tsunesaburō, president of Sōka Kyōiku Gakkai], *Tokkō geppō* [Monthly bulletin of Special Higher Police] (August 1943), 152.

Chapter 5

Occupation, Political Reforms, and Religion

In pre-World War II Japan, religion was used by the government as an element of control in the nation's political and social life. The lack of a universal religion, as discussed in the previous chapters, contributed to the society's vulnerability to the autocratic rule of the emperor and, more specifically, the eventually militaristic government that drew upon his authority.

The 1945 detonation of two atomic bombs in Japan marked the end of World War II and the declaration of Japanese surrender, paving the way for the Allied Powers to rebuild the state through political and religious reforms. This chapter examines Japan's sweeping political and religious changes during the period of occupation. The changes were primarily developed and implemented by the occupiers, despite their initial intent and efforts to let the Japanese political leaders themselves lead the reforms.

This chapter's discussion of the postwar changes often cites the occupiers' official documents, mainly because of their significance in terms of their influence on postwar religion and politics. For example, *Political Reorientation of Japan*, issued in 1950 by the occupation authorities, is referred to in this chapter as a critical document to the extent that it made the real nature of the Japanese prewar Constitution "known for the first time," as Miyazawa Toshiyoshi acknowledges.[1] The same document provides a useful comprehensive analysis of prewar state-religion relations and the political culture of Japan.

A natural counterargument might be that such documents when published by occupation authorities could be propagandic in favor of themselves. However, the content and arguments found in the documents basically align with subsequent research. For example, a collection of letters exchanged between the occupation authorities Supreme Commander Douglas MacArthur and Japan's then prime minister Yoshida Shigeru shows that the head of occupiers suggested on January 3, 1947, that the Japanese government consider constitutional revision. The letter also indicates that MacArthur was willing to allow a national referendum for the revision to take place. However, Yoshida's response was rather ambiguous; he only indicated he would keep MacArthur's proposal in mind.[2] After Yoshida resigned as prime minister and Shinohara Kijūrō succeeded him, the occupation authorities continued attempting to get the Japanese government leaders to revise the Constitution and make it democratic. Eventually, the Japanese government did attempt to revise the Constitution. However, as demonstrated by a recent report published by the Commission on Constitution of the House of Representatives of Japan, the draft of the revised Constitution prepared by the postwar Japanese government leaders essentially maintained the status quo, including the sovereignty of the emperor.[3] The Japanese constitutional drafters regarded the preservation of the emperor's sovereignty as the "grand principle" of the Constitution that they believed should not be changed.[4] This principle, however, was irreconcilable with the concept of democratic sovereignty residing with the people, which the occupation authority sought to establish. The draft prepared by the Japanese was therefore absolutely unacceptable to the occupiers, especially given that the prewar autocracy based on the imperial system had led to Japan's militarism and aggression in the first place. Consequently, the occupation authorities decided to move forward with drafting a new Constitution on their own.

According to the previously cited report recently published by the House of Representatives, MacArthur instructed Prime Minister Shinohara on October 11, 1945, to "democratize the Meiji Constitution."[5] In two weeks, the Japanese government set up a committee for revising the Constitution that was headed by Minister Matsumoto Jōji. On December 8, 1945, Matsumoto stated internally at a legislators' committee meeting that his constitutional drafting would be based on four principles, the first of which being: "No change will be made to the grand principle that the emperor holds the general control of governing authority."[6] On February 2, 1946, details of the draft

Constitution prepared by Matsumoto and his committee, thereafter called the Matsumoto Draft, were scooped and published by the major newspaper *Mainichi Shimbun*. As a result, the "General Headquarters has come to know the outline of the Matsumoto Draft, been surprised by its conservative content, and has decided that the General Headquarters would prepare a constitutional draft on its own."[7] A week after the media broke the story, the Japanese government submitted an outline of its proposed draft to the occupation authorities. The outline was based on the Matsumoto Draft and, therefore, was immediately rejected by the occupiers. On February 13, 1946, the General Headquarters presented the constitutional draft it prepared, so-called the MacArthur Draft, to the Japanese government. The presentation meeting was attended from the Japanese side by Minister Matsumoto, Foreign Minister Yoshida Shigeru, and other government officials. The General Headquarters made clear that the "Matsumoto Committee's proposal is totally unacceptable."[8] The occupiers explained that the General Headquarters instead had prepared a constitutional draft. They requested the Japanese government "make efforts to revise the constitution taking this [MacArthur] Draft into consideration to the maximum extent."[9] The MacArthur Draft "clarified the sovereignty resting with the people, [and] positioned the emperor as a 'symbol.'"[10] The Japanese government officials were "greatly surprised" by the MacArthur Draft and by the occupiers' request to revise the Constitution "in line with" it.[11] The Japanese officials examined the content of the MacArthur Draft and found it deviated substantially from what they considered the constitutional principles. The Japanese government then asked the General Headquarters to consider the Matsumoto Draft again, claiming that it would be more "appropriate for Japan's actual circumstances."[12] The request was, however, "rejected outright" by the occupation authorities.[13] Finally, the Japanese government "decided to prepare its draft based on the [MacArthur] Draft."[14] Verified through the letters between Japan's then prime minister and MacArthur as well as through the recent research conducted by the Japanese government, this report of the process of constitutional drafting is largely consistent with the description of the process appearing in *Political Reorientation* as it will be examined later in this chapter. Thus, *Political Reorientation* is fairer and more genuine in its narratives than as one-sided or propagandic as may be suspected.

As demonstrated in the previous chapters, pre-World War II and wartime Japan was governed through autocracy, where the rule of law did not prevail but rather the rule of man. The situation was so because the emperor was perceived as possessing sovereign power, attained through ancestral inheritance. This condition eventually led to militarism and totalitarian control as the government established State Shinto under the emperor. As demonstrated in the preceding chapter, Shintoism was used by the government to attain its initial objective of expanding its rule to the world and to establish total control of its people. Moreover, most of the religions in Japan supported the militarist government. In this regard, Hardacre is right in stating that "all other branches of Japanese religions up to 1945 had similarly devoted themselves to prayers for military victory, the exaltation of martial spirit, and justification of Japan's supposed mission to rule all of Asia."[15] The fundamental problem was the interrelationship between the use of religion by the militarist authorities and the lack of real resistance from the majority of religions. Although some religious figures tried to resist the government-controlled institutions that forced them to submit to the government, their efforts did not carry an immediate impact because these religious nonconformists suffered persecution or even destruction under the rule of the emperor. Still, the role of State Shinto should be particularly underscored in discussing the issue of religion and state in Japan. After all, it was created by the state authority for the specific purpose of fostering nationalism and later used to support militarism, such as by setting up Yasukuni Shrine and overseas shrines in Asian countries that Japan invaded.

Shinto was used by the government as a tool to control the Japanese until the Potsdam Declaration of Japan's surrender in the war. Japan accepted the Proclamation Defining Terms for Japanese Surrender, popularly known as the Potsdam Declaration, on August 14, 1945. The Potsdam Declaration demanded the elimination of militaristic and totalitarian control and the establishment of democracy, individual freedom, and human rights. Article 4 required Japan to decide "whether she will continue to be controlled by those self-willed militaristic advisers whose unintelligent calculations have brought the Empire of Japan to the threshold of annihilation, or whether she will follow the path of reason."[16] Article 10 reads, "The Japanese Government shall remove all obstacles to the revival and strengthening of democratic tendencies among the Japanese people. Freedom of speech, of religion, and of thought, as well as respect for the fundamental human rights, shall be established."[17]

After surrender, however, the Japanese government still attempted to maintain its prewar and wartime thought-control institutions, including the Maintenance of Public Security Order Law, Special Higher Police and Thought Persecutors. They also sought to continue, for example, the imprisonment and probation of political dissidents under the Maintenance of Public Order Law, as described by Ogino Fujio.[18] These situations triggered the occupation authorities, the General Headquarters of Supreme Commander for the Allied Powers (GHQ), to issue two key directives to remove these institutions. The first directive, the Memorandum for the Removal of Restrictions on Political, Civil, and Religious Liberties, was issued on October 4, 1945. Often referred to as the Human Rights Directive, it ordered the Japanese government to abolish the Maintenance of Public Order Law, Religious Organizations Law, and other legal instruments limiting the freedom of thought, religion, assembly, and speech; grant immediate release to political prisoners; and abolish the thought police.[19] The second directive, the Directive for the Disestablishment of State Shinto from the Supreme Commander of Allied Powers, was issued in December of the same year. Known as the Shinto Directive, it ordered the abolition of state support for Shinto and the separation of religion and government. Furthermore, in January of the following year, GHQ had the emperor issue an imperial rescript renouncing his claim to divinity, which referred to the "false conception that the Emperor is divine and that the Japanese people are superior to other races and fated to rule the world."[20] In November of the same year, the new Constitution was promulgated, with Article 20 guaranteeing freedom of religion and separation of religion and state. The Western occupiers, though presumably to some extent with self-interested motives, tried to form a peaceful, nonmilitaristic, and democratic Japan. In their efforts to do so, the occupation authorities consistently deemed it imperative to separate religion from state and to guarantee religious freedom.

OCCUPATION AUTHORITIES' INITIATIVES AGAINST THE STATE SHINTO–BASED POLITICAL SYSTEM

Occupation authorities led and implemented reforms of Japan's political and constitutional structures including State Shinto. The occupation authorities' headquarters, GHQ, issued directives including the Directive for the Disestablishment of State Shinto from the Supreme Commander of Allied Powers or the "Shinto Directive" that would prevent the government-controlled institutions from providing support to Shinto. Part of the main objective of the Shinto Directive, made explicit in its first article, was to "prevent a recurrence of the perversion of Shinto theory and beliefs into militaristic and ultra-nationalistic propaganda designed to delude the Japanese people and lead them into wars of aggression."[21] GHQ also prepared a memorandum concerning State Shinto on December 3, 1945, shortly before the issuance of the Shinto Directive, which attempted to analyze the problem of State Shinto in relation to Japan's militarism, ultranationalism, and thought control. The analysis of State Shinto presented in this paper, Memorandum on State Shinto to the Chief of Staff, reads:

> State Shinto has been used by militarists and ultra-nationalists in Japan to engender and foster a military spirit among the people and to justify a way of expansion.
>
> Legends analogous to those which have become a vital force in the political and religious life of Japan are common to the early life of many peoples. No other modern nation, however, has attempted to secure social and political cohesion through the strength of a ceremonial nexus that was normal in occidental culture 2,000 to 4,000 years ago. Nor has any other modern religion attempted to utilize such ritualistic agencies for vivifying and achieving the primary ends of national life.
>
> In recent years, Japanese political philosophy has become so closely involved with the Shinto cult that today it can hardly be understood apart from its interconnection with Shinto.
>
> The Japanese were taught that their invincibility in the war was due to their status as a "God-sent race." This idea has played a central part in Japanese military education.

> Not necessarily the most effective, but certainly the most pernicious of the influences working to make State Shinto doctrine all-pervasive was the negative policy of trying to black out every expression of opinion and every thought which might cast doubt upon its validity. For more than twenty years, much effort has been spent on enforcing the official Shinto as a weapon against "dangerous thought." To deny the official mythology was to invite the attention of the thought police and, in some cases, the assassin.[22]

GHQ issued the Shinto Directive on December 15, 1945. It explicitly required the separation of religion and government, stating, "The purpose of this directive is to separate religion from the state, to prevent misuse of religion for political ends, and to put all religions, faiths, and creeds upon exactly the same basis, entitled to precisely the same opportunities and protection."[23] GHQ was determined to abolish State Shinto. Furthermore, the occupation authorities focused on the problem of artificial State Shinto, differentiating it from shrine Shinto as a religion per se. In Sheldon Garon's words, the occupation authorities' "immediate goal was not to disband shrine Shinto as a religion but rather to transform it into a bona fide creed, totally removed from government control."[24] Its focus on State Shinto was, therefore, not necessarily as "distorted" as Hardacre argues.[25] In light of the extreme level of militaristic use of State Shinto by the wartime government, including the imposition of compulsory Shinto worship on the Japanese people for thought-control purposes and the utilization of the formal education system for the dissemination of State Shinto ideology, the relationship between the Japanese state and State Shinto deserves differentiated treatment in terms of academic analysis. The issuance of the Shinto Directive reflected a high-priority reform identified by the occupation authorities as necessary for the comprehensive reorientation of the postwar Japanese state.

The Shinto Directive defined Japan's prewar/wartime system as one based on the "direct or indirect compulsion to believe or profess to believe in a religion or cult officially designated by the state," and State Shinto as "an ideology which has contributed to Japan's war guilt, defeat, suffering, privation and present deplorable condition," and thus required the elimination of these conditions.[26] It sought to "assist the Japanese people in a re-dedication of their national life to building a new Japan based upon ideals of perpetual peace and democracy."[27]

In order to achieve these objectives, the Shinto Directive directed the structural, financial, and personal separation of national and local governments and public education from Shinto.

> The sponsorship, support, perpetuation, control and dissemination of Shinto by Japanese national, prefectural, and local governments, or by public officials, subordinates, and employees acting in their official capacity are prohibited and will cease immediately.
>
> . . .
>
> The dissemination of Shinto doctrines in any form and by any means in any educational institution supported wholly or in part by public funds is prohibited and will cease immediately.[28]

The Shinto Directive also specifically prohibited the circulation of the Fundamental Principles of the National Structure or similar publications: "Circulation by the government of 'The Fundamental Principles of the National Structure' (*Kokutai No Hongi*) . . . and all similar official volumes, commentaries, interpretations, or instructions is prohibited."[29]

Thus, the Shinto Directive pointed out the ideological use of religion by the state as the main factor fueling Japan's militarism and ultranationalism, a claim supported by government actions at the time. Toward the end of World War II, when Japan was losing the war, most of the Japanese people were suffering from deprivation. Still, the wartime government of Japan, where "state power had a strong religious character,"[30] called for the completion of the "holy war" and continued to urge the Japanese people to fight the war. To the same end, the Shrine Board of the Ministry of Home Affairs published *Jinja hongi* or Cardinal Principles of Shinto Shrines in 1944, a booklet prompting the Japanese people to further devote themselves to military causes.[31] According to *Jinja hongi*, "It goes without saying that the military affairs have a close relationship with Shinto shrines."[32] *Jinja hongi* continues on its later pages as follows:

> The path that the Japanese people should follow is absolute obedience to the national polity, which is unparalleled among all nations, thereby supporting the fortune of the emperor, who is eternal like heavens and earths.
>
> . . .

> In this way, the global mission of the Imperial State will be accomplished by allowing all nations to take their places and by extending our divine authority to all peoples throughout the world.[33]

Even after the Allied Powers's air raids devastated Tokyo and other major cities in Japan, the Japanese government leaders continued to encourage the Japanese people to continue their war efforts, claiming that the country would be protected by *kamikaze* or gods' winds. This fanaticism resulted in Japanese leaders refusing to surrender despite the fact that Japan was effectively defeated, which led to the dropping of atomic bombs on Hiroshima and Nagasaki, making the damage of the war even more devastating.[34]

As Garon puts it, the prewar/wartime government ultimately required the "subordination of all religions to the cult of the emperor" and declared State Shinto as the "only religion."[35] Furthermore, as a result of the severe persecution of any religions deviating from the state orthodoxy, more conforming religious groups "rushed to cooperate" with the government's war efforts.[36] Therefore, the Shinto Directive demanded freedom of religion and the separation of religion from the state, as these conditions were imperative to the establishment of peace and democracy. Following the issuance of the Shinto Directive, on December 28, 1945, the Japanese government abolished the Religious Organizations Law, which had been used to control religions and mobilize them for the cause of wars, and instead issued a Religious Corporations Ordinance enabling religious corporations to be founded and registered without having to obtain approval from the state authorities.

OCCUPATION AUTHORITIES' EFFORTS TO PROMOTE RELIGIOUS AND POLITICAL REORIENTATION

The occupation authorities shaped the religious setting and the political arena in Japan through various methods. Along the lines of the Shinto Directive and other initiatives taken by the occupation authorities that demanded the guarantee of religious freedom and the separation of state and religion, the new Constitution of Japan promulgated on November 3, 1946, was a major part of the political reform. Compared to the Meiji Constitution of 1889 that had paid lip service only to the freedom of religious belief by allowing it exclusively "within limits not prejudicial to peace and order and not antagonistic to [the Japanese people's] duties as subjects,"[37] the new Constitution provided "one of the most unconditional guarantees of the freedom of religion in the world."[38]

Political Reorientation, GHQ's report published later in 1950, describes in detail the process of drafting the new Constitution. At the same time, it provides a comprehensive analysis of prewar/wartime Japan's political framework, which the occupation authorities sought to change fundamentally. The model of the Constitution drafted by GHQ aimed at removing the emperor from the sphere of politics and committing the nation of Japan to pacifism, as power was shifted from the emperor to the Diet and cabinet. This marked the beginning of political reorientation in the nation.

The new Constitution included articles on freedom of religion and the separation of religion and state, with Articles 20 and 89, respectively, stipulating as follows:

> Article 20: Freedom of religion is guaranteed to all. No religious organization shall receive any privileges from the state, nor exercise any political authority. No person shall be compelled to take part in any religious act, celebration, rite, or practice. The state and its organs shall refrain from religious education or any other religious activities.
>
> . . .
>
> Article 89: No public money or other property shall be expended or appropriated for the use, benefit, or maintenance of any religious institution or association, or for any charitable, educational, or benevolent enterprises not under the control of public authority.[39]

In addition to these two major Articles of the Constitution, Article 14 forbade the discrimination of people on the basis of politics, economic status, or social relations. Moreover, Article 19 guarantees the protection of the freedom of conscience and thought.

Additionally, the new Constitution of Japan under Article 1 provides a new definition of the emperor as a state symbol and a symbol of unity of the nation whose position derived from the will of the people, depriving him of sovereign power. The same article clarifies that sovereign power lies with the people. This had the overall effect of reducing the emperor from a sacred and inviolable divinity, as was stipulated under the Meiji Constitution, to simply an ordinary human being governed by the rule of law.

The Basis for and Process of Constitutional Revision

Political Reorientation—in its section called the basis for revision—explains the background and rationale for the revision of the Constitution and its drafting by GHQ. This explanation is of particular interest given a persistent claim made even today by some conservative Japanese critics that the new Constitution was one-sidedly imposed by other nations and should be substantially changed. The occupation authorities' description of the drafting process, which as indicated earlier in this chapter proves consistent with the actual facts of drafting verified by the Japanese government, demonstrates otherwise.

The reasons for revising the Constitution involved the provision in regard to freedom of religious belief and the relations between state and religion. Article 28 of the Meiji Constitution of 1889 stated, "Japanese subjects shall, within a limit that is not prejudicial to peace and order, and not antagonistic to their duties as subjects, enjoy the freedom of religious belief."[40] Despite its apparent protection of religious freedom to a reasonable extent, the limit provided in this article in actuality served as an excuse for the prewar/wartime government to restrict freedom and even destroy any religious institutions that the political leaders considered "prejudicial to peace and order" in their discretionary definition. Furthermore, the government made every individual and religious body obliged to accept State Shinto. For this reason, the occupation authorities deemed that Article 28 had permitted ultranationalism and militarism.

Furthermore, the occupation authorities observed that Articles 1 and 3 of the Meiji Constitution portrayed the emperor as an eternal ruler who is inviolable and sacred. The articles in the Constitution are as follows:

> Article 1: The Empire of Japan shall be reigned over and governed by a line of Emperors unbroken for ages eternal.
>
> Article 3: The Emperor is sacred and inviolable.[41]

State Shinto was used to intensify the spirit of militarism in accordance with these articles. Therefore, the occupation authorities found it necessary to revise these articles and redefine the position of the emperor in Japanese society. The Constitution drafted by the occupation authorities deployed the concept of popular sovereignty as stipulated in Article 1 of the new Constitution. Under this article, the emperor would be stripped of the aspect of divinity but would remain a symbol of unity of the Japanese nation.

The process of drafting the new Constitution is described in detail in *Political Orientation*. Referring to *Political Orientation*, Miyazawa emphasizes the significance of its publication, stating:

> The work of studying the revision of the constitution began in October 1945. In January of the following year, a draft, the Matsumoto Draft, was prepared by State Minister Matsumoto. However, the so-called dark change was made in the process, and on March 6, in a seemingly sudden manner, the government's draft outline of the revised constitution, the March 6 Draft, was published.
>
> . . .
>
> There was no information available then at all about what circumstances during the period caused the Matsumoto Draft to disappear and instead gave birth to the March 6 Draft.
>
> . . .
>
> It was [in 1950] that *Political Orientation of Japan* . . . , Supreme Commander MacArthur's report to the government of the United States of America concerning the occupation of Japan, was made public.
>
> . . .
>
> Its Section III, The New Constitution of Japan, clearly explains the sequence of events leading up to the formulation of the March 6 Draft. . . . The dark change in question has been fully brought to light hereto.
>
> . . .
>
> The fundamental nature of the Japanese constitution itself was thus made known correctly for the first time.[42]

Given the elusive nature of the Meiji Constitution, which permitted the rise of militarism and ultranationalism, MacArthur "clearly recognized at the outset that no political reform that did not encompass revision of the constitution would be worth serious consideration."[43] Furthermore, it is noteworthy that, as *Political Reorientation* shows, MacArthur sought to get the Japanese political leaders to take the lead in revising the Constitution.

> During the course of the first 4 months, the Supreme Commander, on several occasions, conveyed to the Japanese government his concern in the matter. It was his basic conception of the Occupation mission that to the fullest possible extent, the Japanese should be permitted and encouraged to do the work and undertake the reforms themselves, under the general guidance and supervision of the Occupation Forces. This concept, certainly a new and liberal one in the annals of military occupations, rose out of his firm belief that that which was imposed by authority or superior military force not only bore the taint of oppression but would be the antithesis of true democracy as well.[44]

Despite MacArthur's expectations, however, the Japanese government's responses turned out to be disappointing. Referring to the Matsumoto Draft, the revision proposed by the Japanese government, *Political Reorientation* reads as follows:

> The proposed revision lags far behind even the most conservative of the unofficial drafts. It is quite apparent that what was hoped was that liberalization of the language of the Meiji Constitution would be acceptable to [the Supreme Commander for the Allied Powers], leaving the real Constitution in its loose and flexible form, open to such application and interpretation as the ruling groups might see fit to apply.[45]

With regard to individual rights, for example, as *Political Reorientation* points out, the Matsumoto Draft, "if anything, reduces the rights and increases the duties of the people."[46] As has been previously demonstrated, the Meiji Constitution included provision for the rights of people but made such rights subject to the provisions of law, thereby allowing the state authorities to restrict and even severely infringe them in essentially discretionary ways. The Matsumoto Draft provided no absolute protection of people's rights, either. In fact, the "Explanation" accompanying the Matsumoto Draft "offers a curious confusion."[47] After referring to situations where people's rights were not respected under the Meiji Constitution but were rather infringed "due to the enactment of evil laws,"[48] the "Explanation" states, "In the draft revision, therefore, it is proposed to insert a general provision to the effect . . . that no restrictions of whatever nature may be imposed upon the freedom and rights of Japanese subjects except by law."[49] Japanese government thus attempted to use the same old tactics that it had used in the Meiji Constitution, enabling it to define and restrict people's freedom and rights discretely. Among many other issues, the Matsumoto Draft indicated no intention to transform the political framework of prewar/wartime Japan that had been based on the rule of man into a new system based on the rule of law. The draft proposed that the power of the emperor should remain intact. The "Explanation" says, "The draft revision proposes to maintain a system where the emperor exercises sovereign power, rather than to adopt a republican form of government with a president at its head, or so-called 'presidential democracy.'"[50] The draft anticipated the power of the emperor to operate "under an Imperial House Law which is not required to be enacted by the Diet."[51] Furthermore, the lack of intent to establish the rule of law was obvious with regard to the very nature of the Constitution. In what follows, *Political Reorientation* describes this problem with the draft:

> There is no provision making the Constitution the supreme law of the land. This omission is, of course, fatal, since it leaves the real Japanese state exactly as it was, and excludes from the operation of law the various extra-constitutional agencies which have been so characteristic a feature of Japanese political structure.[52]

Political Reorientation describes the occupation authorities' disappointment with the Japanese government's responses, as shown in the Matsumoto Draft.

> Faced with the issue of an actual comprehensive revision of the Meiji Constitution, the Matsumoto committee took refuge behind a few vague and substantially meaningless changes in phraseology coupled with an elaborate attempt at justification of their failure to go further.[53]

It then cites an illustrative example of "meaningless changes in phraseology." The Matsumoto Draft proposed replacement of the words "army" and "navy" with "armed forces," with no more substantive changes suggested.[54]

Political Reorientation, in its concluding paragraph on the subsection on the Matsumoto Draft, further emphasizes the occupation authorities' disappointment.

> The Supreme Commander had determined to leave in the hands of the Japanese the fullest possible responsibility for accomplishing the reorganization and liberalization of their government and establishment of the beginnings of a democratic state. On the other hand, the Government, failing completely to respond to the obvious desires and demands of the people of Japan, confirmed in their allegiance to the traditional principles and time-honored customs of the past, indicated little desire to undertake the work, and attempted to resolve the issue with a show of words and a bow in the direction of the West. . . . Their skill in fashioning facades involving no structural remodelling was notable.[55]

In the following month, February 1946, MacArthur ordered the preparation of an answer to the Japanese government, rejecting the Matsumoto Draft. Furthermore, he deemed that a draft Constitution must be prepared by the occupation authorities instead of the Japanese. *Political Reorientation* describes this process as follows:

> It was deemed necessary to reorient the Cabinet on the principles which the Supreme Commander deemed basic.
>
> . . . General MacArthur instructed Brigadier General Whitney, Chief, Government Section, to prepare a detailed answer, rejecting the Matsumoto draft, for submission to the Japanese Government. . . . Further consideration, however, was given . . . by the Supreme Commander, and he finally came to the conclusion that the most effective method of instructing the Japanese Government on the nature and application of these principles would be to prepare a draft constitution.[56]

The occupation authorities' officers met Japanese government representatives on February 13. Informing them that the Matsumoto Draft was "totally unacceptable," the occupation authorities presented the Japanese with a statement prepared in the form of a draft Constitution.[57] After subsequent discussions and meetings, along with consultation with the emperor and his expression of support for the occupation authorities' guidelines, the cabinet eventually drafted a Constitution in line with GHQ's guidance; it was passed by the Diet with minor changes. The new Japanese Constitution was published on November 3, 1946.

The Significance of the New Constitution

The new Constitution was a new dawn for Japan as it established a platform and a legal framework that defined the relationship between religion and the state. The Constitution made a provision for the separation of the state and religion through Article 20, which addressed freedom of religion. Under this article, religious groups were required to operate as private organizations without affiliation to the government. The state, together with its organs, was required to refrain from any activity that would promote state-religion relationships, such as religious education. Admittedly, this Constitution had to be and was drafted by the occupation authorities, and the Japanese had no choice but to accede to it. Nevertheless, this fact does not change the degree to which the Constitution genuinely created an opportunity for Japan to begin creating a more balanced and dynamic relationship between its religions and its society.

Political Reorientation's chapter on the significance of the new Constitution starts with a description of the basic tenets of democracy that the Potsdam Declaration required Japan to establish, such as democratic tendencies among the people; freedom of speech, religion, and thought; and respect for human rights. *Political Reorientation* also reiterates Japan's conventional political culture, which the occupation authorities sought to change: "These [democratic] principles are poles apart from traditional Japanese political philosophy. Clearly, there existed no soil for planting such ideas or the chance for fruitful growth under the Japanese political system."[58] *Political Reorientation* also summarizes the drafting process of the Constitution, including the Japanese government's failure to prepare a satisfactory draft without GHQ's substantial guidance.

> As revolutionary as the changes were, as complete a reorganization as took place, it is not to be looked upon either as a miracle or military fiat. The Japanese Government was told in direct and forthright language that revision of the Constitution was a must if they were to have any hope of meeting the requirements of the Potsdam Declaration. When they failed

> to make even an honest attempt to liberalize the Meiji Constitution, they were given a primer containing the ABCs of modern representative popular government and told to use it as a guide.[59]

The new Japanese Constitution was, In fact, revolutionary. *Political Reorientation* describes its significance as follows:

> The Constitution gives Japan a single, all-embracing organic law, of the land, a thing which it never had before. . . . There can be neither extra-constitutional political institutions nor officers and no officers of the state can be above the law. For the first time in Japanese history, the people can see for themselves not only what their rights and powers are, but what legal limitations are imposed upon the government itself.[60]

The new Constitution proclaimed, in its preamble, that sovereignty resides with the people and, in chapter 1, that the emperor is a symbol without political powers. Chapter 2 renounces war and prohibits armed forces. Chapter 3 corresponds to a bill of rights—rights that are no longer subject to the discretion of the state authorities, as had previously been the case, but that are now absolute and inviolable. *Political Reorientation* says:

> This chapter brings about another major change in the Japanese state, a change which is definite enough on paper but which will take years to make itself felt in Japanese life. By the insertion of a comprehensive and specific guarantee of civil liberties . . . a complete break with the past has been made. . . . Heretofore, every guarantee or privilege pretended to be enjoyed by the subject was limited in fact by the consideration of the state. . . . Today, the individual is given specific vested rights which may not be abridged—the exercise of which may not be interfered with—without his consent.[61]

Given the prewar/wartime unification of State Shinto and government that fueled ultranationalism, it was made certain that Japan would not return to the system. Article 20 of the Constitution stipulates the freedom of religion and separation of government and religion.

> Freedom of religion is guaranteed to all. No religious organization shall receive any privileges from the State, nor exercise any political authority.
>
> No person shall be compelled to take part in any religious act, celebration, rite, or practice.

> The State and its organs shall refrain from religious education or any other religious activity.[62]

In terms of religion and state relations, it is worth noting that in the process of drafting the Constitution, a "prohibition on political activity by religious organizations was deleted as dangerous in the way of giving the government the right to interfere."[63] Attention was thus paid to the establishment of principles to ensure that the new Constitution would serve as a bill of rights, not as a bill restricting and infringing upon them, which the Japanese government at that time was still attempting to preserve.

CONCLUSION: LEGACY OF OCCUPATION

The Allied occupation ended with the Treaty of Peace with Japan, signed in 1951, which came into effect in 1952. The adoption of a new democratic Constitution and relevant political framework alone would not, of course, alter Japan's political culture overnight, and the democratic principles provided in the new Constitution were yet to be substantiated. Yet the new Constitution, at least institutionally, transformed Japan from an autocracy based on the rule of man into a democracy based on the rule of law. This transformation included prohibiting state interference in religious beliefs and practices.

The change had to be made by the occupation authorities, however, because the Japanese government lacked any serious intention to bring about a fundamental change and instead only pursued superficial changes in order to preserve the prewar/wartime regime. It was only as "a last resort" that this approach to the transformation was taken.[64] For the sake of today's political discussion, while Japan ultimately had no option other than to follow the instructions of the occupation authorities after having lost the war, it is of interest to emphasize that the new Constitution was not completely imposed by the Allied Powers, as is argued by today's conservative politicians and other critics in the country. Its drafting by GHQ was made inevitable by the Japanese government leaders' refusal to rewrite the Constitution themselves in good faith. More importantly, imposed or not, the new Constitution succeeded in liberalizing religious and other individual rights in Japan.

NOTES

1. Miyazawa Toshiyoshi, *Kenpō kaisei* [Constitutional revision] (Tokyo: Yuhikaku Publishing, 1956), 4. All quotations from Miyazawa are the author's translations unless stated otherwise.

2. Sodei Rinjirō, comp. and trans., *Yoshida Shigeru—MacArthur ōfuku shokanshū [1945–1951]* [Collection of correspondences between Yoshida Shigeru and MacArthur] (Tokyo: Hosei University Press, 2000), 166–67.

3. House of Representatives of Japan, *Nihonkoku kenpō no seiteikatei ni kansuru shiryō* [Materials on the enactment process of the constitution of Japan] (Tokyo: The Secretariat, Commission on Constitution, the House of Representatives, 2016), 1–2. All quotations from House of Representatives of Japan, Commission on Constitution are the author's translations unless stated otherwise.

4. House of Representatives, *Seiteikatei* [Enactment process], 2.

5. House of Representatives, *Seiteikatei* [Enactment process], 2.

6. House of Representatives, *Seiteikatei* [Enactment process], 2.

7. House of Representatives, *Seiteikatei* [Enactment process], 2.

8. House of Representatives, *Seiteikatei* [Enactment process], 3.

9. House of Representatives, *Seiteikatei* [Enactment process], 3.

10. House of Representatives, *Seiteikatei* [Enactment process], 3.

11. House of Representatives, *Seiteikatei* [Enactment process], 3.

12. House of Representatives, *Seiteikatei* [Enactment process], 3.

13. House of Representatives, *Seiteikatei* [Enactment process], 3.

14. House of Representatives, *Seiteikatei* [Enactment process], 3.

15. Helen Hardacre, *Shinto: A History* (New York: Oxford University Press, 2017), 444.

16. Proclamation Defining Terms for Japanese Surrender (Potsdam Declaration), issued July 26, 1945, https://history.state.gov/historicaldocuments/frus1945Berlinv02/d1382 (May 2, 2023).

17. Potsdam Declaration.

18. Ogino Fujio, *Shisō kenji* [Thought prosecutors] (Tokyo: Iwanami Shoten, 2000), 185.

19. General Headquarters of Supreme Commander for the Allied Powers, *Memorandum for the Removal of Restrictions on Political, Civil, and Religious Liberties*, October 4, 1945.

20. Emperor of Showa, "Chokusho" [Imperial rescript], *Kanpō* [Government gazette], special issue (January 1, 1946): 1.

21. General Headquarters of Supreme Commander for the Allied Powers, *Directive for the Disestablishment of State Shinto*, December 15, 1945.

22. General Headquarters of Supreme Commander for the Allied Powers, *Memorandum on State Shinto to the Chief of Staff*, December 3, 1945.

23. General Headquarters, *Disestablishment of State Shinto*.

24. Sheldon Garon, *Molding Japanese Minds: The State in Everyday Life* (Princeton: Princeton University Press, 1997), 208.

25. Hardacre, *Shinto*, 444.

26. General Headquarters, *Disestablishment of State Shinto*.

27. General Headquarters, *Disestablishment of State Shinto*.

28. General Headquarters, *Disestablishment of State Shinto*.

29. General Headquarters, *Disestablishment of State Shinto*. As described in introduction and chapter 3, there are a variety of English translations of the title *Kokutai no nongi*. The translation used in the Shinto Directive is "The Fundamental Principles of the National Structure" as quoted.

30. Murakami Shigeyoshi, *Gendai shūkyō to seiji* [Contemporary religions and politics] (Tokyo: University of Tokyo Press, 1978), 77. All quotations from Murakami are the author's translations unless stated otherwise.

31. The English title of and all quotations from *Jinja hongi* are the author's translations unless otherwise stated.

32. Ministry of Home Affairs, *Jinja hongi* [Cardinal principles of shinto shrines] (Tokyo: Printing Bureau, June 1944), 129.

33. Ministry of Home Affairs, *Jinja hongi* [Cardinal principles of shinto shrines], 132–33.

34. Murakami, *Gendai shūkyō to seiji* [Contemporary religions and politics], 30.

35. Garon, *Molding Japanese Minds*, 85.

36. Ogino Fujio, *Tokkō keisatsu* [Special higher police] (Tokyo: Iwanami Shoten, 2012), 111.

37. Emperor of Meiji, *Dainihon Teikoku Kenpō* [The Constitution of the Empire of Japan], promulgated February 11, 1889, trans. Ito Miyoji, https://www.ndl.go.jp/constitution/e/etc/c02.html (May 1, 2023).

38. Garon, *Molding Japanese Minds*, 208.

39. Imperial Diet, *Nihonkoku Kenpō* [The Constitution of Japan], 90th Imperial Diet, promulgated November 3, 1946, https://www.japaneselawtranslation.go.jp/ja/laws/view/174 (May 2, 2023).

40. Emperor of Meiji, *Dainihon Teikoku Kenpō* [The Constitution of the Empire of Japan].

41. Emperor of Meiji, *Dainihon Teikoku Kenpō* [The Constitution of the Empire of Japan].

42. Miyazawa, *Kenpō kaisei* [Constitutional revision], 1–4.

43. General Headquarters of Supreme Commander for the Allied Powers, *Political Reorientation of Japan: September 1945 to September 1948—Report of Government Section, Supreme Commander for the Allied Powers* (Washington, DC: US Government Printing Office, 1949), 90.

44. General Headquarters, *Political Reorientation*, 90–91.

45. General Headquarters, *Political Reorientation*, 99.
46. General Headquarters, *Political Reorientation*, 100.
47. General Headquarters, *Political Reorientation*, 100.
48. General Headquarters, *Political Reorientation*, 100.
49. General Headquarters, *Political Reorientation*, 100.
50. General Headquarters, *Political Reorientation*, 99.
51. General Headquarters, *Political Reorientation*, 99
52. General Headquarters, *Political Reorientation*, 100.
53. General Headquarters, *Political Reorientation*, 100–101.
54. General Headquarters, *Political Reorientation*, 101.
55. General Headquarters, *Political Reorientation*, 101.
56. General Headquarters, *Political Reorientation*, 101–102
57. General Headquarters, *Political Reorientation*, 105.
58. General Headquarters, *Political Reorientation*, 112.
59. General Headquarters, *Political Reorientation*, 113.
60. General Headquarters, *Political Reorientation*, 113.
61. General Headquarters, *Political Reorientation*, 114–15.
62. Imperial Diet, *Nihonkoku Kenpō* [The Constitution of Japan].
63. General Headquarters, *Political Reorientation*, 104.
64. State-War-Navy Coordinating Committee of the US Government, *Reform of the Japanese Government System*, January 7, 1946, https://history.state.gov/historicaldocuments/frus1946v08/d116 (May 2, 2023).

Chapter 6

Religious Decline in Postwar Japan and the Cost of Contemporary Japan's Religious Culture

Japan's defeat in World War II brought about drastic political changes, including the establishment of a constitutional guarantee of religious freedom, as described in the preceding chapter. Ironically, however, the country was faced with a religious vacuum, with the post-World War II economic reconstruction leading to the urbanization and secularization of the society in general.

This chapter focuses first on the religious decline in Japan after the war, reviewing how both conventional and new religions responded to the new circumstances and the attempted revival of religious control by state authorities. Second, it examines the political involvement of Sōka Gakkai as the religion with the largest electoral influence, discussion of which offers an insight into the government's attempt to increase its control over religion. The chapter then examines Japan's contemporary sociopolitical culture as it relates to the religious situation. Last, the chapter considers the implications of Japan's religion and state relations and political culture for the postsecular world, although this examination is more suggestive than exhaustive.

RELIGIOUS DECLINE IN POSTWAR JAPAN

Despite religious freedom having been guaranteed under the new Constitution, as described earlier, most religions in Japan have either declined or only grown to a limited extent since the end of World War II. According to a survey conducted by NHK Broadcasting Culture Research Institute, over 60 percent of Japanese people do not follow a particular religion. Furthermore, the percentage of the people who said they have a "sense of faith" declined from 32 percent in 1998 to 26 percent in 2018.[1] Thus, despite religious freedom being finally secured after World War II, religious sentiment has remained largely undeveloped among the Japanese.

The current status of Shinto shrines has been illustrative of this religious vacuum. After World War II, the National Association for Shrines (NAS) considered shrines to serve a crucial function in creating a bond between the Japanese people and the sun goddess, the imperial institution, and the imperial myth.[2] However, a survey conducted by the NAS in 2007, cited by Breen and Tween,[3] proved that the NAS's thinking was very different from the local people's understanding of the shrines. The main areas of engagement with the shrines were for the new year ceremony, during prayers for family well-being, and during celebrations related to rites of passage, such as the newborn's first shrine visit and the traditional celebration of children reaching the ages of three, five, and seven. None of the respondents "cited imperial, patriotic themes as a reason for visiting their local shrine."[4] Furthermore, the survey indicated that the majority of Japanese people had little knowledge about their local shrine.

The lack of religious knowledge among the Japanese implies that, although the Japanese show a strong inclination toward rituals, they do not have a great interest in religious doctrine. The NAS took the initiative to promote religion, attempting to create an interest in shrines among the Japanese by selling amulets at the local shrines.[5] The amulets are believed to be sacred objects where the sun goddess resides. The NAS used them to draw a connection between religion and shrines in a bid to create some knowledge of doctrine in the Japanese. However, people could not use the amulets in the absence of altars. In response, the shrine officers in Japan distributed altars for free to the people at the local shrines as well as through "local volunteers knocking on doors."[6] Nevertheless, these efforts have not produced any meaningful results, and Shinto has in fact declined significantly since World War II, with only 3 percent of the Japanese population having faith in Shinto.[7]

The decline of Shinto, as Hardacre described, is partly attributable to demographic urbanization coupled with "the increasingly secular disposition of the society, the growing prestige of science (seen by most as antithetical to religion of any kind), and the media's tendency to ignore or ridicule religion."[8] Another factor contributing to the decline of Shinto's religious legitimacy is the "commercialization of the shrines,"[9] which was a step taken with the aim of helping them survive financially in the absence of state patronage. Larger shrines have built wedding halls, where Shinto weddings are conducted in combination with Christian or other Westernized ceremonies for the same couple. Similarly, many of the Shinto shrines have survived by promoting shrine visits on New Year's Day to make a once-a-year wish with monetary offerings. Shrines in commercial areas encouraged merchants to visit them to make financial contributions and, in return, to receive "good luck." Thus, the role of Shinto in society has been reduced to the commercial and, at best, customary. The lack of philosophical or metaphysical underpinnings of Shinto has only reinforced this. As Hardacre bluntly puts it, "commercialization of the shrines contributes to society's impression of Shinto as ethically and intellectually bankrupt."[10] There has been no sign of reversal of this declining trend in Shinto.

Similarly, conventional or temple Buddhism has weakened significantly since the end of World War II. During World War II, thousands of urban temples were severely damaged in air raids. They also lost many of their parishioners in the same air raids or due to their evacuation to other areas of the country. Temples in rural areas, too, lost most of their financial base. Before World War II, temples often owned substantial farmland that they leased to local farmers. However, the postwar land reform, which was ordered by the occupation authorities and implemented as part of the political and economic reforms, transferred land ownership from the landlords to the farmers. The land reform caused temple Buddhism's parishioner system to weaken as well. Parishioner leadership was typically in the form of advantaged farmers who used to own farmland and lease it to other farmers, but the reform substantially deprived them of land ownership.

On the other hand, the head temples of many schools of Buddhism maintained their financial base because they owned mountains and forests that were not subject to the agricultural land reform and thereby secured forestry as their financial source. The disproportionate financial base of the head temples, in contrast to other temples, led to the centralization of power within the respective schools of conventional Buddhism and to the development and maintenance of an authoritarian culture in the Buddhist school.

Many Buddhist temples also turned to tourism for additional revenue by, for example, advertising their architecture and well-maintained gardens without emphasizing religious aspirations or essential transcendence. These tendencies only confirmed and reinforced the established character of temple Buddhism as *sōshiki bukkyō*, or funeral Buddhism.

Japanese Christianity showed only limited growth, despite financial and missionary support provided by churches in other countries. The establishment of many private universities and schools affiliated with Christian churches did not substantially increase followers. According to statistics published every year by the Japanese government, the Christian population has remained at approximately 1 percent of the total Japanese population to date since 1949 when the post-World War II Japanese government began conducting numerical studies on religions.[11] This is partly attributable to the fact that most Japanese Christian churches had accepted the prewar/wartime State Shinto system to avoid persecution. They had thereby failed to demonstrate their religious commitment that was necessary to appeal to the Japanese people who were looking for a legitimate source of empowerment in the aftermath of the war. Also, although accepted by intellectuals and the urban middle-class population to some extent, few Japanese churches conducted proactive evangelical activities on a grassroots basis.

Though older traditions failed to expand, one growing segment of the Japanese religious community was that of the so-called new religions. For example, Ōmotokyō and Hitonomichi Kyōdan, both of which had experienced persecution by the wartime government, were rebuilt after World War II. Risshō Kōseikai, a spinoff group from a religion founded in 1919 called Reiyūkai, also developed into a sizeable group. However, the new religions, which generally tended to be cults based on the founder's allegedly "supernatural" personality, did not appeal to intellectuals. They were seen as incompatible with science, which was becoming Japan's mainstream approach to addressing the societal agenda, and hence they gained only limited social or political influence.

SŌKA GAKKAI'S POLITICAL INVOLVEMENT

After the war, the lay Nichiren Buddhist group Sōka Gakkai was rebuilt by Toda Jōsei, Makiguchi's disciple, who had survived imprisonment. The Buddhist sect caused disruption in both the Japanese religious and political landscapes. In fact, it offers an interesting example of a religion actively promoting a moral vision to the government. However, this example also indicates that getting involved in politics exposes a religious group to the risk of becoming a mere vote-gathering machine and losing its fundamental religious nature.

Sōka Gakkai began to get involved in politics in 1955 when, after forming its own political department, it sponsored and saw elected to office fifty-three candidates in local elections. In the national Upper House election in the following year, three of its members were elected. Sōka Gakkai's decision to enter politics was initially made by Toda, who had experienced the wartime suppression of the organization, his own imprisonment, and the death of his mentor. Richard Seager, following an exhaustive study of literature and fieldwork about Sōka Gakkai, provides a balanced assessment of the group's motives and the critics' views.

> The difference between Toda's intent in revitalizing the Gakkai and the Japanese public's perceptions of its goal and spirit was the source of much of the intense controversy that marks the movement's history. Toda saw the movement as a progressive force in building a new Japan in a post-war . . . age, its spirit forged in Makiguchi's resistance to State Shinto, and the two men's experience of repression and imprisonment. He understood the Gakkai's right to pursue this goal aggressively, moreover, as secured by the new constitution.
>
> But Toda's, and later Ikeda's, critics often came to view things very differently.[12]
>
> Toda's intent was to build a movement that turned the poisons of post-war crises into spiritual and political medicine. Much of the controversy this generated can, in retrospect, be traced to profound ambiguities in the postwar situation. . . . Defeat, rapid reconstruction, and the Cold War, moreover, created a highly fluid, often volatile social situation. In this

> context, the Gakkai's well-coordinated and highly successful propagation campaigns could, quite understandably, spell danger, particularly in a society that, unlike the United States, had little experience with high-energy evangelization.[13]

After Toda's death in 1958, his successor Ikeda Daisaku established a political party called Kōmeitō, or the Clean Government Party, in 1964. Kōmeitō's rapid growth in its early days alarmed the public, invited significant skepticism about its motives from both the domestic and international media, and, naturally, instigated pressures from its political opponents. Today, however, Kōmeitō has gained recognition as a major player in the Japanese political system, becoming the third-largest political party in Japan and part of the two-party ruling coalition, together with the Liberal Democratic Party (LDP), the country's largest party. The following comment given to the *Financial Times* by Koike Yuriko, the governor of Tokyo and former LDP legislator, provides a perspective:

> When Yuriko Koike was asked at the beginning of Japan's general election campaign who should be prime minister if her party won the vote, she replied: "I think Natsuo Yamaguchi would be good." She was referring to the low-profile leader of Kōmeitō, the centrist party, which is the long-term coalition partner to prime minister Shinzo Abe's much larger Liberal Democratic party. . . . Her open courting of Mr. Yamaguchi reveals much about his party's influence over Japanese politics. Kōmeitō has, over the past five years, helped bring stability to Mr. Abe's government while also preventing the prime minister from shifting too far from the centre. Yet with its roots in Sōka Gakkai, the Buddhist religious movement, Kōmeitō will also be the main constraint on Mr. Abe's ability to deliver on his election promises, including to revise Japan's pacifist constitution.[14]

It should be recalled, nevertheless, that it took Kōmeitō decades to gain this status. Its early growth since its inception in the mid-1960s triggered the state power holders to try to revive religious controls to weaken the party's electoral base, especially before Kōmeitō joined the ruling coalition in 1999. As Garon writes, there have been "major movements to revive aspects of prewar managerial policies toward religions."[15] For example, LDP attempted several times to introduce legislation to make Yasukuni Shrine a state-supported institution. The

Religious Corporation Law (RCL) was revised in December 1995 to grant the government greater powers of supervision over religious bodies, despite the opposition of most major religious groups, from the United Church of Christ to the Kyoto Buddhist Association. Among the provisions of this act were a shift in authority over religious organizations from the local to the central government, and increased government access to religious organizations' records. The government asserted that the revision was part of an effort to prevent criminal activities such as Aum Supreme Truth's sarin gas attack on the Tokyo metropolitan subway in March 1995. However, the real motives for revising the RCL were more political than they were genuine. This primary purpose was candidly acknowledged by Kamei Shizuka, an LDP spokesperson, when he told a television audience that the purpose of revising the law was "to take measures against Sōka Gakkai,"[16] which at the time endorsed Kōmeitō as an opposition party. In fact, legal recognition of the Aum cult as a religious corporation had been terminated by the court in October 1995, prior to the revision of the law. Thus, Aum was never governed by the revised RLC. Metraux points out the irrelevance of the revision of RLC for controlling terrorism.

> The Aum incident demonstrated that the Japanese government lacks an adequate security mechanism to prevent a terrorist incident by a group well armed with poison gas and imported weapons. A more appropriate reaction might have been to improve the accountability of the nation's security system against terrorists—for which revision of the Religious Corporation Law is really irrelevant.[17]

After the LDP lost a majority in the Lower House election in 1993 and significantly decreased its number of seats in the Upper House in 1998, it requested that Kōmeitō join the ruling coalition in July 1999. The LDP's pressure on the Buddhist group has since decreased dramatically. Prior to 1999 when the coalition was formed, the LDP was antagonistic toward Kōmeitō and Sōka Gakkai. That this antagonism stemmed from political reasons is proven by the fact that, after the coalition was formed, it stopped trying to act against them.

At the same time, in the background of Kōmeitō's growth exist not only political circumstances but also Sōka Gakkai's transformation. Ikeda's emphasis on human development through both religious and intellectual approaches has especially facilitated the Buddhist group's development into an established part of society. Ikeda also founded universities, high schools, elementary schools, and kindergartens whose curricula are as secular as other private and public educational institutions. The founding of educational institutions was also an extension of Makiguchi's hybrid approach to human development based on education and religion. Seager highlights the significance of Ikeda's dialogues and publications with the world's leading intellectuals, starting with the historian Arnold Toynbee, stating that they marked "further steps both in [Ikeda's] personal education and the Gakkai's maturation."[18] Ikeda's awareness of the importance of dialogue is also expressed in his own words. In a serial story of the history of Sōka Gakkai that Ikeda contributed to the *Seikyō Shimbun* newspaper, he writes, "If religion closes the window on dialogue, it will fall into a labyrinth of self-righteous dogmatism and authoritarianism. Dialogue is what makes religion alive among people."[19] These factors also suggest that the sustainability of Sōka Gakkai's future growth depends on its continuous efforts to incorporate intellectual engagement into its grassroots movement.

In terms of relations between religion and politics, Sōka Gakkai's growth provides an unprecedented case in Japan where a religious organization independent of state authority has grown into a politically influential segment of the society through the establishment and endorsement of a political party that has become part of the ruling coalition. If one considers its presence in the Diet, Kōmeitō holds only thirty-two out of the 465 total seats in the House of Representatives, as of August 1, 2022. This is somewhat marginal compared to its coalition partner LDP, holding 261, which enables LDP as the largest party to control the Lower House independently. Thus, its number of seats alone does not fully explain the influence of Kōmeitō in this coalition.

A major reason why LDP keeps Kōmeitō in its coalition, despite frequent policy compromises LDP must make, is the electoral support provided by Kōmeitō's supporters to LDP members in constituencies where no Kōmeitō candidates are running. Under Japan's two-tier electoral system, voters cast one ballot choosing a candidate in single-member constituencies and a second choosing a political party in eleven regional proportional representation blocks. As coalition partners, LDP and Kōmeitō have agreed not to run candidates against one another in single-member districts. In exchange, Kōmeitō requests its supporters, mainly Sōka Gakkai members, to vote for LDP candidates, while the LDP is expected to ask its supporters in certain districts to vote for Kōmeitō. LDP understands that it benefits from this arrangement. In exchange for helping LDP secure votes for its candidates, a critical factor especially in tight races, Kōmeitō retains its position as an indispensable ruling coalition partner.[20] As a party championing pacifism, Kōmeitō has often leveraged its influence by acting as a "brake" on the LDP's more hawkish ambitions. In one case,

> Kōmeitō forced (now former) Prime Minister Shinzo Abe's administration to accept that collective self-defense would be permitted only in a limited number of circumstances. It has also thwarted the push by the LDP conservatives to replace Article 9, the postwar constitution's famed "peace clause," with more permissive language.[21]

Kōmeitō also demonstrated its pacifist stance when Sōka Gakkai International president Ikeda published an "urgent proposal" to the 2020 Review Conference of the Parties to the Treaty on the Non-Proliferation of Nuclear Weapons, including an appeal to allow no first use of nuclear weapons by nuclear powers.[22] In response to a question asked at a press briefing by a reporter from the national broadcaster NHK regarding this proposal, Kōmeitō leader Yamaguchi said, "our party takes it seriously and will discuss it."[23] Furthermore, Kōmeitō has represented grassroots voices, including those of housewives, small businesses, and other ordinary members of society. Policies that Kōmeitō has successfully negotiated with LDP include maintaining a reduced-consumption tax rate on household staples, advocating for reduced-schooling fees, and offering child allowances.[24] In these ways, Kōmeitō, supported by Sōka Gakkai, echoes the kind of checks-and-balances relationship between politics and faith-based groups found in other democracies. Nakano Tsuyoshi finds value in the Buddhist group's involvement in the political sphere, stating, "The Sōka Gakkai's political participation created new trends in the political realm and encouraged greater interest in and willingness to participate in politics and other public spheres."[25] Nakano describes Sōka Gakkai's political involvement as an "effort to find a new way for religion, which had been pushed into the inner realm of the individual under modern secularism, to make a social and political contribution."[26]

The basic idea behind Sōka Gakkai entering politics was for them to have the opportunity to protect their own religious freedom, following the prior suppression that the group's leaders had experienced during World War II. However, Sōka Gakkai now faces the risk of losing part of its universal or transcendent nature as a Buddhist group due to its affiliation with a political party. Nakano also points out the risk that Sōka Gakkai's involvement in political spheres could erode its own religious principles.

> Characteristics of religious principles, even when they are applied to socio-political purposes, are that they represent universal principles for humanity and highly abstract ideas. When religion upholds its ideals and gets involved in politics to reform government or state, there is a high risk that its essential religious ideas could be tarnished in the midst of a collision of interests in the real world if religion is absorbed into real-life power politics.[27]

Sōka Gakkai leadership seems to be aware of this risk. In 2004, the group's then president Akiya Einosuke stated:

> [The Kōmeitō] party has upheld a consistent principle of conducting political activities from people's perspectives, including tackling welfare issues based on its founding spirit of respecting human life. We expect the party to continue to do so. If it deviates from this principle, I think we should even consider an option to discontinue our support for the Kōmeitō or other parties. We have our own stance. We need not or have no reason to be used for politics.[28]

Nevertheless, addressing the risk associated with its involvement in Japanese politics remains a major challenge for Sōka Gakkai's future growth. If the group weakens its checks-and-balances attitude, its organizational endorsement of part or all of the ruling coalition could reduce its grassroots movement to simply a vote-gathering machine.

THE COST OF CONTEMPORARY JAPAN'S RELIGIOUS APATHY

The religious apathy of the overwhelming majority of the Japanese population is reflected in the country's sociopolitical culture—especially in the context of what Karel Wolferen refers to as "the absence of a tradition appealing to transcendental truth or universal values."[29] The absence of such a tradition is especially conspicuous when viewed against the backdrop of reduced deference toward democratic values, such as the rule of law and respect for human rights and civil society.

The Allied Powers's occupation authorities, as described in the preceding chapter, implemented major policies to transform Japan into a democracy, including helping establish the new Constitution on the basis of the rule of law. The transformation has been successful to a significant extent; however, there remain loopholes. A major loophole is *gyōseishidō,* or administrative directives, the executive branch's directives issued without explicit legislative grounds. For example, the Ministry of Education, Culture, Sports, Science, and Technology has consistently instructed public schools to have their students and teachers sing "Kimigayo" (Reign of the Emperor), a song composed in 1880, as a de facto national anthem. It was only in 1999, however, that legislation related to the national anthem was completed with the passing of the Law Regarding the National Flag and National Anthem. However, the administrative instruction to sing "Kimigayo" did not change with the passage of this legislation. Furthermore, even the aforementioned law does not provide explicitly stated rules that require schools to sing the national anthem. The executive branch thus exercises its power without specific legal grounds. The ability of the government to use administrative discretion in this way is concerning, as it illustrates undermining of the rule of law.

Kawashima Takeyoshi attributes the Japanese tendency to undermine the rule of law to the lack of "ought-ness in laws," or a tension "between ideals and realities."[30] Compared to the Western philosophy of law, where laws must pursue what is right, laws in Japan are still considered a set of rules imposed by power holders. Kawashima relates this problem to the lack of transcendent religious tradition in Japan, describing a comparison with European religious tradition: "The idea of dualism between ideals and realities is not unique to laws but underlies European religions . . . and the dualistic idea concerning laws perhaps represents only an aspect of this philosophical tendency."[31] Unlike in Europe and some other civilizations, Japan has generally lacked a religious tradition that fosters transcendent thinking. The lack of a dualistic understanding that incorporates both ideals ("oughtness") and realities, pointed out by Kawashima, derives from this lack of transcendent ideas. As a result, laws in Japan are essentially understood not as instruments that represent what is right but rather as a set of rules issued by decision makers.

The popular conception of human rights in Japan shows that Japanese society lacks a tradition of appealing to transcendent ethical principles. For instance, Nakaya Yasuko, a Christian, protested the enshrinement of her late husband, who had died after serving with the Self-Defense Force (SDF), at a Shinto shrine. Her objections, based on her own and her late husband's personal religious beliefs, were "difficult even for some of her neighbors and relatives to understand. Someone who wants to be, or appears to be, different and who takes an independent stand, is generally perceived as abnormal."[32] Nakaya's legal complaint filed against the SDF was dismissed by the Supreme Court. Hardacre criticizes the court decision.

> In denying Nakaya Yasuko's claim to have such a right, the high court interpreted the problem as a conflict between her religious freedom and that of the shrine. This way of framing the question imputed person-hood to the shrine and then reasoned that the shrine was free to memorialize anyone as it saw fit. . . . The Supreme Court's failure to rule on the religious character of deification rites enabled politicians to continue to patronize Yasukuni and to lobby for the reestablishment of state support.[33]

Despite the constitutional guarantee, understanding of the concept of human rights remains superficial in Japan. As Noda Yoshiyuki observes, "For the average Japanese, this word [rights] conjures up something related to egoism."[34]

The neglect of individual rights in Japan is also evident in light of the international system. Japan is one of the few member-states of the United Nations not to have adopted any of the individual complaint mechanisms established in international human-rights treaties and their optional protocols—the mechanisms that enable individuals to complain about the violation of their rights in an international arena.

Another example of disrespect for human rights in Japan, which as discussed earlier as essentially related to the lack of religiously grounded transcendent thinking, is how the country treats its national minorities. The minority issue is illustrated in the current status of the Ainu, the indigenous people of northern Japan. Although the Ainu Cultural Promotion Act was passed in 1997 recognizing the Ainu presence, "it did not grant the Ainu any significant or specific legal instruments that could counter their material and ideological marginalization which has resulted from almost half a millennium of oppressive colonial rule."[35]

The neglect of human rights in Japan is related to the Japanese government's state-centric mindset, which occasionally gets manifested in its incompetence in protecting the security of its residents. In fact, such a mindset took precedence over the safety of the country's people after the devastating earthquake and tsunami that hit the northeastern part of Japan on March 11, 2011, and the subsequent nuclear power plant accidents. For instance, the Japanese government under the Kan Naoto administration declined the US government's immediate offer to, among other things, have the US Air Force stationed in Japan supply effective coolant to prevent anticipated nuclear meltdowns, as Kan's own party admitted.[36] The administration instead opted for the much less effective method of spraying seawater over the nuclear facilities, with Prime Minister Kan himself hovering in a helicopter over the affected region in what was widely perceived to be a political show. These insufficient cooling measures resulted in nuclear meltdowns, hydrogen-air explosions, and the release of radioactive materials.

The underdevelopment of civil society is also related to this state-centric tendency. In Wolferen's words appearing in the *New York Times*, "'civil society'—the part of the body politic outside the active Government and power system—is virtually unknown in Japan."[37] Although legislation concerning civil-society organizations, the Act on Promotion of Specified Non-Profit Activities, was enacted in 1998, the law prohibits nonprofit organizations (NPOs) from conducting any political activities. Furthermore, no major civil or political movement has emerged to challenge this prohibition despite the possibility that the law violates the Constitution, especially Article 21, which guarantees the "freedom of assembly and association as well as speech, press, and all other forms of expression."[38] As Wolferen defines it in the previously cited newspaper article, civil society is important as a part of politics not directly linked to the system of power. Japanese civil society's response to disasters is mostly hindered by this regulation, which prohibits NPOs from conducting activities that may have some political affiliations. The underdevelopment of civil society in Japan, as in the case of the neglect of human rights, is partly caused by the lack of appeal to religious transcendence that empowers the people to act independently from the state. Building a transcendent tradition in

Japan could, therefore, help enhance the protection of human rights and promote the growth of civil society.

IMPLICATIONS FOR GLOBAL GOVERNANCE

The problems with Japanese political culture discussed in this chapter, such as its cultural and political disrespect for human rights and the underdevelopment of its civil society partly due to the lack of a tradition of appealing to religious transcendency, have implications for global governance, which is dominated to a large extent by geopolitics and market forces.

A useful analysis is offered by Richard Falk, who presents the interrelationship between religion and global governance, although he does not break down problems specific to Japan. He sheds some light on the role of religion in helping establish humane global governance, while providing a suggestive measure that religious leaders and organizations can take to avoid exploitation by the authorities. He states that "the quality of democracy depends on the orientation of political culture as much as constitutional forms and practices."[39] An appropriate world order is needed to solve persistent global problems, such as economic gaps and environmental deterioration, but it remains elusive. Falk describes the kind of global governance emerging in today's world as contributing to "global inhumane governance"[40] and calls for the "role of religion as a way of . . . 'humanizing' globalization by the advocacy of a global ethic,"[41] while recognizing the "double-edged relevance of religion,"[42] the negative side of which refers to religious extremism and the opportunistic use of religion by power holders. In response to examples of religious authority invoked for legitimizing the act of war, Falk suggests a format for more positive contributions to be made by religion.

> If organized religion is to achieve spiritual authority, it must respond independently to state power, unwavering in its commitment to peacefulness and justice, as well as dedicated to the pursuit of spiritual goals in public as well as private space. These spiritual goals need to accord with widely endorsed ethical goals such as the avoidance of war, the mitigation of poverty, struggles against oppression, and campaigns to restore and maintain nature, and safeguard the sanctity of life.[43]

Falk clarifies what he means by religion.

> It is evident that religion cannot be reduced to any single religious tradition, although it can draw strength from the collaborative support of the various traditions, and that some aspects of certain religious traditions are antithetical, especially claims of being "the chosen people" or the exclusive or superior instruments of a divine or sacred design or of the enactment of some apocalyptic scenario for ascent to a higher form of existence.[44]

Falk provides a rationale for his emphasis on the role of religion, stating that "the religious awakening can contribute to the formation of identities that . . . can foster from positions of deep rootedness an understanding and celebration of a transcendent common humanity."[45] To develop a type of global governance that counterbalances that centered on geopolitics and market forces and cannot be achieved by the United Nations, he calls for religion's contribution.

> The religious challenge is to infuse the struggle of the peoples of the world for democracy, equity, and sustainability with a vision of human existence that is human-centered yet conscious of the relevance of the sacred and of mysteries beyond the grasp of reason and machines.[46]

While he offers guidance, one problem with Falk's argument is that it does not offer any concrete recommendations. In the case of Japan, the underdevelopment of democratic values and culture, as seen in this chapter, reflects the lack of a transcendent moral tradition. Therefore, a solution could be the establishment of such a tradition that could be developed by religion independent of state authority. As Maruyama suggests, "without the establishment of value standards independent from political values, political liberty is ultimately dependent on political power relations."[47]

CONCLUSION

Despite the freedom of religion guaranteed under the new Constitution, most new and conventional religions in Japan have remained socially uninfluential. Sōka Gakkai may present an unprecedented case in terms of its sociopolitical influence, although its involvement in the Japanese political process poses a risk of it being reduced to a vote-gathering machine unless its checks-and-balances function against state authority is consistently maintained. The attempted revival of religious control by state authorities reflects Japanese political culture, which has tended to suppress those autonomous religious movements that have developed over centuries and hence cannot be easily transformed into a truly democratic culture. This political culture is mirrored by the underdevelopment of democratic values in Japan, including the rule of law, human rights, and civil society.

This chapter has also considered the possible implications of the case of Japan for global governance in terms of relations between religion and state. The state-centric political culture of Japan provides an example of a society where human-centric values remain undeveloped partly due to the lack of a tradition of appealing to religious transcendence. This view resonates with the argument of Falk, who emphasizes the importance of the role of transcendent religion in establishing ethical values independent from political and economic interests, though the geographical scope of this book's discussion branches off from Falk's own arguments toward building humane global governance.

NOTES

1. Kobayashi Toshiyuki, "Nihonjin no shukyōteki ishiki ya kōdō wa dō kawattaka" [How have the Japanese people's religious awareness and behaviors changed?], *Hōsōkenkyū to chōsa* [Broadcasting research and surveys], (April 2019): 53.
2. John Breen and Mark Teeuwen, *A New History of Shinto* (Hoboken: John Wiley & Sons, 2010), 203.
3. Breen and Teeuwen, *New History*, 203–4.
4. Breen and Teeuwen, *New History*, 204.
5. Breen and Teeuwen, *New History*, 203.
6. Breen and Teeuwen, *New History*, 204.
7. Kobayashi, "Nihonjin no shukyōteki ishiki" [Japanese people's religious awareness], 53.
8. Helen Hardacre, *Shintō and the State, 1868–1988* (Princeton: Princeton University Press, 1989), 142.
9. Hardacre, *Shintō and the State*, 143.
10. Hardacre, *Shintō and the State*, 142.

11. Agency for Cultural Affairs, “Shūkyō tōkei chōsa” [Statistical survey on religions], n.d., https://www.bunka.go.jp/tokei_hakusho_shuppan/tokeichosa/shumu/index.html (May 3, 2023).

12. Richard Seager, *Encountering the Dharma: Daisaku Ikeda, Soka Gakkai, and the Globalization of Buddhist Humanism* (Berkeley: University of California Press, 2006), 53–54.

13. Seager, *Encountering the Dharma*, 55.

14. Robin Harding, “Coalition Partner Keeps Japan’s Abe in Power—And in Check,” *Financial Times*, October 17, 2017, https://www.ft.com/content/feed704c-b31e-11e7-a398-73d59db9e399 (May 3, 2023).

15. Sheldon Garon, *Molding Japanese Minds: The State in Everyday Life* (Princeton: Princeton University Press, 1997), 206.

16. Kamei Shizuka, *Sunday Project*, aired October 22, 1995, Asahi National Broadcasting.

17. Daniel Metraux, “The Aum Shinrikyo Incident, Revision of the Religious Corporation Law and the Debate over the Separation of Church and State in Contemporary Japan” (paper presented at Japan Seminar, Washington, DC, April 26, 1996).

18. Seager, *Encountering the Dharma*, 119.

19. Ikeda Daisaku, “Shin ningen kakumei” [New human revolution], *Seikyo Shimbun*, August 13, 2016, 3. All quotations from Ikeda are the author’s translations unless stated otherwise.

20. Tobias Harris and Levi McLaughlin, “The Small Pacifist Party That Could Shape Japan’s Future,” *Foreign Policy*, November 4, 2021, https://foreignpolicy.com/2021/11/04/komeito-ldp-japan-elections-defense-policy-china/ (May 3, 2023).

21. Harris and McLaughlin, “Small Pacifist Party.”

22. Ikeda Daisaku, “NPT saikentō kaigi eno kinkyū teian” [Urgent proposal to the NPT Review Conference], *Seikyō Shimbun*, July 26, 2022.

23. Yamaguchi Natsuo, “Regular Press Briefing by the Representative of Kōmeitō,” July 26, 2022, video of briefing, https://www.youtube.com/watch?v=J8U0G15_tA4 (May 3, 2023).

24. Harris and McLaughlin, “Small Pacifist Party.”

25. Nakano Tsuyoshi, *Sengo Nihon no shūkyō to seiji* [Religion and politics in postwar Japan] (Tokyo: Taimeido, 2003), 204. All quotations from Nakano are the author’s translations unless stated otherwise.

26. Nakano, *Shūkyō to seiji* [Religion and politics], 204.

27. Nakano, *Shūkyō to seiji* [Religion and politics], 199–200.

28. Akiya Einosuke, “Sōka Gakkai kaichō Akiya Einosuke intabyū” [Interview with Akiya Einosuke, the president of Sōka Gakkai], interview by Kappei Kawamura, *Aera* (February 2, 2004): 26–27. All quotations from Akiya are the author’s translations unless stated otherwise.

29. Karel Wolferen, *The Enigma of Japanese Power* (Tokyo: Charles E. Tuttle Co., 1993), 317.

30. Kawashima Takeyoshi, *Nihonjin no hō ishiki* [Japanese people's legal consciousness] (Tokyo: Iwanami Shoten, 1967), 43. All quotations from Kawashima are the author's translations unless stated otherwise.

31. Kawashima, *Hō ishiki* [Legal consciousness], 43.

32. David O'Brien, *To Dream of Dreams: Religious Freedom and Constitutional Politics in Postwar Japan* (Honolulu: University of Hawaii Press, 1996), 143.

33. Helen Hardacre, *Shinto: A History* (New York: Oxford University Press, 2017), 472.

34. Noda Yoshiyuki, *Introduction to Japanese Law* (Tokyo: University of Tokyo Press, 1976), 159.

35. Giorgio Shani, *Religion, Identity and Human Security* (New York: Routledge, 2014), 163.

36. AFP-BB News, "Fukushima genpatsu jiko: Nihon seifu beigawa shien kotowaru—Yomiuri Shimbun" [Fukushima nuclear powerplant accident: Japanese government turns down the U.S.' offer to help—according to Yomiuri Shimbun], March 18, 2011, https://www.afpbb.com/articles/-/2791010 (May 3, 2023).

37. Karel Wolferen, "America and Japan: 50 Years Later; An Economic Pearl Harbor?" *New York Times*, December 2, 1991, https://www.nytimes.com/1991/12/02/opinion/america-and-japan-50-year-later-an-economic-pearl-harbor.html (May 3, 2023).

38. Imperial Diet, *Nihonkoku Kenpō* [The Constitution of Japan], 90th Imperial Diet, promulgated November 3, 1946, https://www.japaneselawtranslation.go.jp/ja/laws/view/174 (May 3, 2023).

39. Richard Falk, *Religion and Human Global Governance* (New York: Palgrave, 2001), 162.

40. Falk, *Religion*, 17.

41. Falk, *Religion*, 75.

42. Falk, *Religion*, 16.

43. Falk, *Religion*, 114.

44. Falk, *Religion*, 29.

45. Falk, *Religion*, 8.

46. Falk, *Religion*, 33.

47. Maruyama Masao, *Maruyama Masao kōgiroku* [The lectures of Maruyama Masao], vol. 6 (Tokyo: University of Tokyo Press, 2000), 128–29.

Conclusion

This book has, in the first two chapters, reviewed some region- and country-specific paradigms of state and religion relationships and provided case studies on religion's position in foreign policies and domestic politics, demonstrating both positive and negative interactions between religions and state authorities. These initial examinations have provided a global and comparative context for the later discussions specific to Japan.

In the rest of the chapters, the book has argued that various governments in Japan, from the early modern period through World War II, have either manipulated or marginalized religions within its borders and stripped them of their transcendent values. Early modern authorities regularly employed religion as a means of achieving local political goals. They refused to countenance the idea of religion as an appeal to universal values by which one might criticize (or at least gain an alternate perspective on) local political goals or current power arrangements. Against this backdrop, the modern period's power holders created a religion of state worship to drive nationalism and eventually militarism in order to fight World War II. Any other sense of religion as an appeal to universal values outside of emperor worship was marginalized and persecuted as heretical. After the war, the Allied Powers's occupation authorities drafted a democratic constitution for the country, one that included freedom of religion and the separation of religion and state. However, lacking a tradition of universal religiosity independent of local authorities, postwar Japanese society has remained largely secular.

This is because, unlike many other democracies in the world, there have been few healthy checks and balances relations between the state and religion in Japan. This has been a factor in the underdevelopment of democratic political culture, despite the aforementioned post-World War II Japanese Constitution that provides one of the strongest protections of religious freedom in the world. This problem aligns with the perspective of reconstructive postmodernism, which has served as a theoretical framework for this book, in that developing a positive reconstruction of the relationships between secularity and religiosity is considered imperative for achieving democratic and humane governance.

On the other hand, as we have seen in the previous chapters, there have also been religious movements in different eras that attempted to overcome this tendency and establish independent spiritual bases. However, most of them failed to wield sufficient social or political influence and eventually were neutralized by the power holders through persecution or otherwise incorporation into the political system. After World War II and the establishment of the new Japanese Constitution, there have been religious movements that have gained a certain level of political influence by forming their own political parties and providing them with electoral support. Questions about such movements include whether the religious organizations directly involved in the political process can maintain their transcendent values independent from the state without becoming simply vote-gathering machines that provide blind, faith-based support to their political arm. To avoid this situation, such a religious organization must seek to constantly reevaluate its own political stance and determine whether or not it is compromising its core values for political purposes.

Furthermore, reconstructing a healthy relationship between the state and religion requires a checks and balances relationship between secularity and religiosity. Religions can serve to prevent the absolutization of state power, while human intellect can check the dogmatization of religions. To this end, religious bodies should seek third-party advice, including from intellectuals not only in Japan but in various countries with diverse intellectual, cultural, and religious backgrounds. In short, reconstructing the productive relationship between religiosity and secularity necessitates maintaining a balance between transcendent spirituality and human intellect.

Moreover, if religion is to contribute to the humanizing of global governance by acting independently from state power and religious extremism as expected from the perspective of reconstructive postmodernism, cooperation among different religious traditions is needed to form a kind of solidarity that will benefit mankind. In actuality, however, religion is fragmented, not only among different religious traditions, but also within individual religions. Such fragmentation only increases the vulnerability of a given religion to the forces that attempt to manipulate it. Establishing spiritual authority, therefore, necessitates interreligious dialogue and collaboration.

Interreligious dialogues, however, also face their own challenges. Various attempts by international forums to encourage interreligious/civilizational dialogues have failed to produce any significant outcomes. At interreligious dialogues, in Kohara Katsuhiro's words, "representatives from religions gather often only to perfunctorily confirm the importance of peace, tolerance, and coexistence without exchanging any substantive discussions."[1]

In fact, as Giorgio Shani demonstrates, neither a resolution issued by the United Nations General Assembly in 2001 on the Global Agenda for Dialogue among Civilizations, which reaffirms member-states' "commitment to the fulfilment of Universal Declaration of Human Rights as a common standard of achievement for all peoples and nations," nor the UN Alliance of Civilizations, established in 2005, has achieved meaningful progress.[2] Fundamentally problematic with these UN-sanctioned initiatives is the fact that they are initiated by states, while the value of interreligious dialogue lies in religion's independence from state authority. In Shani's words, "The establishment of an alliance based on key nation-states acting as civilizational representatives has done little to challenge the state-centric ontology of international relations, which itself dates from the secular settlement at the Peace of Westphalia."[3] A dialogue institutionalized by states is contradictory in its nature to the expected role of religion, which is to be independent of state authority. Only when interreligious dialogues are autonomously conducted can they substantiate values that represent diverse cultures and at the same time benefit humanity. A more prospective approach is therefore nongovernmental interreligious dialogues with a focus on the human agenda. The launch of the Asia Pacific Faith-Based Coalition for Sustainable Development, announced in March 2018, may provide an example of such an initiative, although its outcome has yet to be seen.

Another problem with the aforementioned UN General Agenda is, as Shani points out, its presumed "universality."[4] A universal approach alienates people with different traditions and beliefs as it often papers over meaningful differences in its efforts to reach consensus. On the other hand, cultural relativism tends to be unresponsive to shared global and human problems and therefore makes little positive contribution to the objectives of interreligious dialogue. What is needed in international dialogue is, in Shani's words, "to respect, yet not essentialize, the alterity of the 'other' and not to try to assimilate the 'other' to the 'self.'"[5] Constructive religious dialogue applies an inclusive approach, where different traditions' belief systems are respected while an attempt is made to identify human commonalities.

In terms of international human rights law, for example, interreligious dialogues should aim to cultivate values independent from political values. Rather than seeking alignment based on existing legal texts, they should pursue transformation of the global political culture and a shift from rule by military and economic power to the rule of law. The emphasis on international human rights law would then become more relevant, including the law's dual roles of representing the sanctity of individuals beyond state authority and safeguarding the rights of individuals against infringement committed in the name of religion. In Falk's words, human rights law could "receive civilizational and social ratification as well as a formal acceptance at the level of government."[6] International human rights law, in other words, provides not a universal standard but rather a useful starting point for interreligious dialogue.

Furthermore, meaningful interreligious dialogue necessitates substantial interactions with and input from academic experts, not only in religious subjects but also in secular fields. Interreligious dialogues incorporating intellectual expertise could help prevent religious self-righteousness and dogma from undermining the objectives of dialogues by incorporating more diverse perspectives and free thinking. Meaningful interreligious dialogues, as Kohara states, "leverage scientific knowledge that mankind has fostered to ensure an adequate understanding of human commonalities."[7] On a regional level, such efforts are being promoted to some extent by, for example, the European Academy of Sciences and Arts, a transnational and interdisciplinary network of experts in science, art, and religion. Enhancement of these and other nongovernmental regional initiatives and interactions among them on a global scale are instrumental in producing meaningful results from interreligious/civilizational dialogues. Further, the maintenance of such dialogues is crucial to the continued development of Japanese society.

Since the end of World War II, Japan has rapidly developed into an economic power under the new democratic constitution. However, democratic values have remained underdeveloped in Japanese political culture. In terms of religion-state relations, what has been seen consistently throughout Japan's history is a lack of religiously inspired ethical values independent of secular state authorities. On the other hand, religious movements have sought to overcome this state-centric political culture by providing religious inspiration to the people. In the past, however, such movements were either destroyed by state authorities or neutralized through incorporation into the power structure. Today, even under the democratic constitution, the same challenge faces religious movements that seek to establish transcendent ethical values among the people. Overcoming the challenge would necessitate consistent self-checking and self-reforming efforts with an awareness of the risk of political manipulation, as well as open-minded, intellectual dialogues with a wide range of external parties such as academics, other religious groups, philanthropic practitioners, and business leaders.

A global implication of this study of Japan's religion-state relations is that, in the postsecular world, developing human-centric global governance necessitates substantive dialogue and collaboration among religions and between the religious and the secular. Only through such dialogues can religion be a positive force in shifting the world's political principles from rule by military and economic power to the rule of law. The dialogues should be sufficiently inclusive to admit differences and sufficiently responsible to seek to identify human commonalities that deserve respect and protection.

NOTES

1. Kohara Katsuhiro, "Nikushimi no bunka wo koete" [Beyond the culture of hatred], *Seikyo Shimbun*, April 28, 2018, 3.

2. Giorgio Shani, *Religion, Identity and Human Security* (New York: Routledge, 2014), 102–3.

3. Shani, *Religion*, 103.

4. Shani, *Religion*, 103.

5. Shani, *Religion*, 104.

6. Richard Falk, *Religion and Humane Global Governance* (New York: Palgrave, 2001), 8.

7. Kohara, "Nikushimi no bunka" [Culture of hatred], 3.

Bibliography

AFP-BB News. "Fukushima genpatsu jiko: Nihon seifu beigawa shien kotowaru—Yomiuri Shimbun" [Fukushima nuclear powerplant accident: Japanese government turns down the U.S.' offer to help—according to Yomiuri Shimbun]. March 18, 2011. https://www.afpbb.com/articles/-/2791010 (May 3, 2023).

Agency for Cultural Affairs. "Shūkyō tōkei chōsa" [Statistical survey on religions]. n.d. https://www.bunka.go.jp/tokei_hakusho_shuppan/tokeichosa/shumu/index.html (3 May 2023).

Aizawa, Hisashi. *Gendai kokka ni okeru shūkyō to seiji* [Religion and politics in the contemporary states]. Tokyo: Keiso Shobo, 1966.

Akiya, Einosuke. "Sōka Gakkai kaichō Akiya Einosuke intabyū" [Interview with Akiya Einosuke, the president of Sōka Gakkai]. Interview by Kappei Kawamura, *Aera* (February 2, 2004).

Anderson, John. "Putin and the Russian Orthodox Church: Asymmetric Symphonia?" *Journal of International Affairs* 61, no. 1 (Fall/Winter 2007): 186. http://www.jstor.org/stable/24358086 (May 11, 2023).

Balmer, Randall. "The Real Origin of the Religious Right." *Politico Magazine*, May 27, 2014. https://www.politico.com/magazine/story/2014/05/religious-right-real-origins-107133/ (May 10, 2023).

BBC. "Christianity in Britain." https://www.bbc.co.uk/religion/religions/christianity/history/uk_1.shtml (May 5, 2023).

Beauchamp, Zack. "Juche, the State Ideology That Makes North Koreans Revere Kim Jong Un, Explained." *Vox*, June 18, 2018. https://www.vox.com/world/2018/6/18/17441296/north-korea-propaganda-ideology-juche (May 5, 2023).

Bebbington, David. "Religion and National Feeling in Nineteenth-Century Wales and Scotland." In *Religion and National Identity*, edited by Stuart Mews. Oxford: Basil Blackwell, 1982.

Bellah, Robert N. "Civil Religion in America." *Daedalus* 96, no. 1 (1967): 1–21. https://www.jstor.org/stable/20027022 (May 5, 2023).

Black, John. *Reign of Elizabeth (1558–1603)*. Oxford: Clarendon Press, 1949.

Breen, John, and Mark Teeuwen. *A New History of Shinto*. Hoboken: John Wiley & Sons, 2010.

Brownlee, John S. "Four Stages of the Japanese Kokutai (National Essence)." Paper presented at the Japan Studies Association of Canada Conference, October 2000. https://www.adilegian.com/PDF/brownlee.pdf (May 13, 2023).

Brzezinski, Zbigniew. *Power and Principle*. Toronto: McGraw-Hill Ryerson, 1983.

Butler, John. "Coercion, Miracle, Reason: Rethinking the American Religious Experience in the Revolutionary Age." In *Religion in a Revolutionary Age*, edited by Ronald Hoffman and Peter J. Albert, 63–69. Charlottesville: The University Press of Virginia, 1994.

Canellos, Peter S., and Josh Gerstein. "'Operation Higher Court': Inside the Religious Right's Efforts to Wine and Dine Supreme Court Justices." *Politico*, July 8, 2022. https://www.politico.com/news/2022/07/08/religious-right-supreme-court-00044739 (May 10, 2023).

Carpenter, Ted G. "Many Predicted NATO Expansion Would Lead to War. Those Warnings Were Ignored." *Guardian*, February 28, 2022. https://www.theguardian.com/commentisfree/2022/feb/28/nato-expansion-war-russia-ukraine (May 11, 2023).

Carter, Jimmy. *Faith: A Journey for All*. New York: Simon & Schuster, 2018.

Carter, Jimmy. *Inaugural Address of President Jimmy Carter*. January 20, 1977. https://www.jimmycarterlibrary.gov/assets/documents/speeches/inaugadd.phtml (May 9, 2023).

Catto, Rebecca, Grace Davie, and David Perfect. "State and Religion in Great Britain: Constitutional Foundations, Religious Minorities, the Law and Education." *Insight Turkey* 17, no. 1 (Winter 2015): 79–96.

Committee for Compiling Chronological Records of Makiguchi Tsunesaburō and Toda Jōsei, eds. *Nenpu Makiguchi Tsunesaburō Toda Jōsei* [Chronological records of Makiguchi Tsunesaburō and Toda Jōsei]. Tokyo: Daisanbunmeisha, 1993.

Committee on Foreign Affairs, House of Representatives. *Religious Persecution in the Soviet Union (Part II): Hearing before the Subcommittee on Europe and the Middle East and on Human Rights and International Organizations of the Committee on Foreign Affairs, House of Representatives; Ninety-Ninth Congress, Second Session, 30 July 1986*. Washington, DC: US.Government Printing Office, 1986.

Cornell Law School. "Establishment Clause." https://www.law.cornell.edu/wex/establishment_clause (May 5, 2023).

Covell, Stephen. *Japanese Temple Buddhism: Worldliness in a Religion of Renunciation*. Honolulu: University of Hawaii Press, 2005.

Cuaresma, Jesus Crespo, Olha Danylo, Steffen Fritz, Martin Hofer, Homi Kharas, and Juan Carlos. "What Do We Know About Poverty in North Korea?" *Palgrave Communications* 6, no. 40 (2020): 1–8. https://doi.org/10.1057/s41599-020-0417-4 (May 15, 2023).

Curtice, John, Elizabeth Clery, Jane Perry, Miranda Phillips, and Nilufer Rahim, eds. *British Social Attitudes: The 36th Report*. London: The National Centre for Social Research, 2019. https://www.bsa.natcen.ac.uk/ (May 5, 2023).

Diamant, Jeff. "With High Level of Prayer, U.S. Is an Outlier Among Wealthy Nations." Pew Research Center website, May 1, 2019. https://www.pewresearch.org/fact-tank/2019/05/01/with-high-levels-of-prayer-u-s-is-an-outlier-among-wealthy-nations (May 5, 2023).

Dumke, David. "P-I Focus: Bush Weds Religion, Politics to Form World View." *Seattle Post-Intelligencer*, August 21, 2004. https://www.seattlepi.com/local/opinion/article/P-I-Focus-Bush-weds-religion-politics-to-form-1152104.php (May 10, 2023).

Emperor of Meiji. *Dai-Nihon Teikoku Kenpō* [The Constitution of the Empire of Japan], promulgated February 11, 1889. Translated by Itō Miyoji. https://www.ndl.go.jp/constitution/e/etc/c02.html (May 2, 2023).

Emperor of Showa. "Chokusho" [Imperial rescript], *Kanpō* [Government gazette]. Special issue (January 1, 1946).

European Parliament Think Tank. "Russia's War on Ukraine: The Religious Dimension." April 1, 2022. https://www.europarl.europa.eu/RegData/etudes/ATAG/2022/729355/EPRS_ATA(2022)729355_EN.pdf (May 11, 2023).

Fagan, Geraldine. "How the Russian Orthodox Church Is Helping Drive Putin's War in Ukraine." *Time*, April 25, 2022. https://time.com/6167332/putin-russian-orthodox-church-war-ukraine/ (May 11, 2023).

Falk, Richard. *Declining World Order*. New York: Routledge, 2004.

Falk, Richard. *Religion and Humane Global Governance.* New York: Palgrave, 2001.

Fraser, Giles. "Putin's Spiritual Destiny." *The London School of Economics and Political Science Religion and Global Society Blog*, February 25, 2022. https://blogs.lse.ac.uk/religionglobalsociety/2022/02/putins-spiritual-destiny/ (May 11, 2023).

Froese, Paul. "Forced Secularization in Soviet Russia: Why an Atheistic Monopoly Failed." *Journal for the Scientific Study of Religion* 43, no. 1 (2004): 35–50. http://www.jstor.org/stable/1387772.

Fukuyama, Francis. "The Modernizing Imperative: The USSR as an Ordinary Country." *The National Interest*, no. 31 (1993): 10–18. http://www.jstor.org/stable/42894852.

Garon, Sheldon. *Molding Japanese Minds: The State in Everyday Life.* Princeton: Princeton University Press, 1997.

General Headquarters of Supreme Commander for the Allied Powers. *Directive for the Disestablishment of State Shinto*. December 15, 1945.

General Headquarters of Supreme Commander for the Allied Powers. *Memorandum for the Removal of Restrictions on Political, Civil, and Religious Liberties*. October 4, 1945.

General Headquarters of Supreme Commander for the Allied Powers. *Memorandum on State Shinto to the Chief of Staff*. December 3, 1945.

General Headquarters of Supreme Commander for the Allied Powers. *Political Reorientation of Japan: September 1945 to September 1948—Report of Government Section, Supreme Commander for the Allied Powers*. Washington, DC: US Government Printing Office, 1949.

Gilbert, John. "Jimmy Carter's Human Rights Policy and Iran: A Re-examination, 1976-79." *Madison Historical Review* 5, Article 1 (2014): 1-25. https://commons.lib.jmu.edu/mhr/vol5/iss1/1/ (September 18, 2023).

Hall, Robert, ed. *Kokutai No Hongi: Cardinal Principles of the National Entity of Japan.* Translated by John Gauntlett. Cambridge: Harvard University Press, 1949.

Halpin, Dennis P. "North Korea's Kim Family Cult: Roots in Japanese State Shinto?" *NK News*, February 19, 2015. https://www.nknews.org/2015/02/north-koreas-kim-family-cult-roots-in-state-shinto/ (May 5, 2023).

Hamid, Shadi. "America Without God." *Atlantic*, March 10, 2021. https://www.theatlantic.com/magazine/archive/2021/04/america-politics-religion/618072/ (May 10, 2023).

Hardacre, Helen. *Shinto: A History.* New York: Oxford University Press, 2017.

Hardacre, Helen. *Shintō and the State, 1868–1988*. Princeton: Princeton University Press, 1989.

Harding, Robin. "Coalition Partner Keeps Japan's Abe in Power—And in Check." *Financial Times*, October 17, 2017. https://www.ft.com/content/feed704c-b31e-11e7-a398-73d59db9e399 (May 3, 2023).

Harris, Tobias, and Levi McLaughlin. "The Small Pacifist Party That Could Shape Japan's Future." *Foreign Policy*, November 4, 2021. https://foreignpolicy.com/2021/11/04/komeito-ldp-japan-elections-defense-policy-china/ (May 3, 2023).

Helgesen, Geir. "Political Revolution in a Cultural Continuum: Preliminary Observations on the North Korean 'Juche' Ideology." *Asian Perspective* 15, no. 1 (1991): 187–213. http://www.jstor.org/stable/42705297 (May 15, 2023).

Holden, Michael. "Young British People Want to Ditch the Monarchy, Poll Suggests." *Reuters*, May 21, 2021. https://www.reuters.com/world/uk/young

-british-people-want-ditch-monarchy-poll-suggests-2021-05-20/ (May 5, 2023).

Holmes, George. *The Oxford History of Medieval Europe*. Oxford and New York: Oxford University Press, 2001.

Holt, James. "John: King of England." *Encyclopedia Britannica*. https://www.britannica.com/biography/John-king-of-England/Quarrel-with-the-church (May 5, 2023).

Home Ministry. "Sōka Kyōiku Gakkai kaichō Makiguchi Tsunesaburō ni taisuru jinmon chōsho bassui" [Excerpts from the records of interrogation of Makiguchi Tsunesaburō, president of Sōka Kyōiku Gakkai]. *Tokkō geppō* (Monthly bulletin of Special Higher Police) (August 1943): 137–61.

Hoshino, Seiji. *Kindai Nihon no shūkyō gainen* [The concept of religion in modern Japan]. Tokyo: Yūshisha, 2012.

House of Peers. *Dai 74-kai Teikoku Gikai Kizokuin Shūkyō Dantaihōan Tokubetsu Iinkai gijiroku dai ichi gō* [The minutes of the meeting of Special Committee on Religious Organizations Bill, House of Peers, the 74th Session of the Imperial Diet, no. 1]. January 25, 1939. https://teikokugikai-i.ndl.go.jp/minutes/api/emp/v1/detailPDF/img/007401484X00119390125 (April 24, 2023).

House of Representatives of Japan. *Nihonkoku kenpō no seiteikatei ni kansuru shiryō* [Materials on the enactment process of the constitution of Japan]. Tokyo: The Secretariat, Commission on Constitution, the House of Representatives, 2016.

Hurley, Lawrence, and Andrew Chung. "U.S. Supreme Court Overturns Roe v. Wade, Ends Constitutional Right to Abortion." *Reuters*, June 28, 2022. https://www.reuters.com/world/us/us-supreme-court-overturns-abortion-rights-landmsark-2022-06-24/ (May 10, 2023).

Ikeda, Daisaku. "NPT saikentō kaigi eno kinkyū teian" [Urgent proposal to the NPT Review Conference]. *Seikyō Shimbun*, July 26, 2022.

Ikeda, Daisaku. "Shin ningen kakumei" [New human revolution]. *Seikyo Shimbun*, August 13, 2016.

Imperial Diet. *Chian Iji Hō* [Maintenance of Public Order Law]. Legislation No. 46 of 1925. 50th Imperial Diet. Promulgated April 22, 1925. https://www.digital.archives.go.jp/img/1643344 (April 24, 2023).

Imperial Diet. *Chian Iji Hō Kaisei Hō* [Act to Revise the Maintenance of Public Order Law]. Legislation No. 54 of 1941. 76th Imperial Diet. Promulgated March 8, 1941. https://www.digital.archives.go.jp/img/147953 (April 24, 2023).

Imperial Diet. *Nihonkoku Kenpō* [The Constitution of Japan]. 90th Imperial Diet, promulgated November 3, 1946. https://www.japaneselawtranslation.go.jp/ja/laws/view/174 (May 2, 2023).

Imperial Diet. *Shūkyō Dantai Hō* [Religious Organizations Law]. Legislation No. 77 of 1939. 74th Imperial Diet. Promulgated April 8, 1939. https://www.digital.archives.go.jp/img/137999 (April 26, 2023).

Inoue, Kowashi. "Shūkyō no jiyū nitsuki ikensho" [Opinion on freedom of religion]. Written 1884. In *Nihon kindai shisō taikei* [A compendium of modern Japanese thoughts], Vol. 5, *Shūkyō to kokka* [Religion and state], edited by Yasumaru Yoshio and Miyachi Masato, 70–75. Tokyo: Iwanami Shoten, 1988.

Jefferson, Thomas. "Jefferson's Letter to the Danbury Baptists." 1802. https://www.loc.gov/loc/lcib/9806/danpre.html (May 5, 2023).

Josephson, Jason. *The Invention of Religion in Japan*. Chicago: University of Chicago Press, 2012.

Kakubayashi, Fumio. *Nihon kodai no seiji to eizai* [Politics and economy in Japan's ancient period]. Tokyo: Yoshikawa Kobunkan, 1998.

Kamei, Shizuka. *Sunday Project*. Aired October 22, 1995. Asahi National Broadcasting.

Kamen, Henry. *Early Modern European Society*. New York: Routledge, 2000.

Kawashima, Takeyoshi. *Nihonjin no hō ishiki* [Japanese people's legal consciousness]. Tokyo: Iwanami Shoten, 1967.

Kenryō, Minowa. "Gendai Nihon bukkyo no tokuchō" [Characteristics of contemporary Japanese Buddhism]. *Bulletin of the Faculty of Letters of Aichi Gakuin University* 38 (2008): 345–64.

Khazanov, Anatoly M. "Marxism-Leninism as a Secular Religion." In *The Sacred in Twentieth-Century Politics*, edited by Roger Griffin, Robert Mallett, and John Tortorice, 119–42. London: Palgrave Macmillan, 2008. https://doi.org/10.1057/9780230241633_7 (May 2, 2023).

Kim, Sookyung, Kyu-chang Lee, Kyung-ok Do, and Jea-hwan Hong. *White Paper on Human Rights in North Korea 2019*. Seoul: Korean Institute for National Unification, 2019. https://www.kinu.or.kr/main/eng (May 5, 2023).

Kobayashi, Toshiyuki. "Nihonjin no shūkyōteki ishiki ya kōdō wa dō kawattaka" [How have the Japanese people's religious awareness and behaviors changed?]. *Hōsōkekyū to chōsa* [Broadcasting Research and Surveys] (April 2019): 52–72.

Kohara, Katsuhiro. "Nikushimi no bunka wo koete" [Beyond the culture of hatred]. *Seikyo Shimbun*, April 28, 2018.

Kowalewski, David. "Protest for Religious Rights in the USSR: Characteristics and Consequences." *Russian Review* 39, no. 4 (October 1980): 426–41. https://www.jstor.org/stable/128810 (May 15, 2023).

Kuroda, Toshio. "Shinto in the History of Japanese Religion." Translated by James Dobbins and Suzanne Gay, *Journal of Japanese Studies*, vol. 7, no. 1 (1981): 1–21.

Kramer, Stephanie. "Religious Composition of India." Pew Research Center, September 21, 2021. https://www.pewresearch.org/religion/2021/09/21/religious-composition-of-india/ (May 5, 2023).

Lee, Grace. "The Political Philosophy of Juche." *Stanford Journal of East Asian Affairs* 3, no. 1 (Spring 2003): 105–12. http://www.asia-studies.com/sjeaa2003.html (May 5, 2023).

Lee, Kyu-chang, Sookyung Kim, Ji Sun Yee, Eun Mee Jeong, and Yejoon Rim. *White Paper on Human Rights in North Korea 2020.* Seoul: Korean Institute for National Unification, 2020. https://www.kinu.or.kr/main/eng (May 5, 2023).

Maan, Eman Atta. "The Hindu-Muslim Conflict Under Modi." *Traileoni*, March 26, 2021. https://traileoni.it/2021/05/the-hindu-muslim-conflict-under-modi/ (May 5, 2023).

MacAskill, Ewen. "George Bush: 'God Told Me to End the Tyranny in Iraq.'" The Guardian, October 7, 2005. https://www.theguardian.com/world/2005/oct/07/iraq.usa (10 May 2023).

Maizland, Lindsay. "India's Muslims: An Increasingly Marginalized Population." Council on Foreign Relations. https://www.cfr.org/backgrounder/india-muslims-marginalized-population-bjp-modi (May 5, 2023).

Makiguchi, Tsunesaburō. *Jinsei chirigaku* [Human geography]. First edition. Tokyo: Bunkaido Shoten, 1903.

Makiguchi, Tsunesaburō. *Jinsei chirigaku* [Human geography]. Eighth edition. Tokyo: Bunkaido Shoten, 1908.

Makiguchi, Tsunesaburō. *Sōka kyōikugaku taikei* [A system of value-creating education]. Vol. 2. Tokyo: Fuzanbo, 1931.

Maruyama, Masao. *Maruyama Masao kōgiroku* [The lectures of Maruyama Masao]. Vol. 4. Tokyo: University of Tokyo Press, 1998.

Maruyama, Masao. *Maruyama Masao kōgiroku* [The lectures of Maruyama Masao]. Vol. 6. Tokyo: University of Tokyo Press, 2000.

Maruyama, Masao. *Thought and Behavior in Modern Japanese Politics.* London: Oxford University Press, 1969.

Maxey, Trent. *The "Greatest Problem": Religion and State Formation in Meiji Japan.* Cambridge: Harvard University Asia Center, Harvard University Press, 2014.

MacAskill, Ewen. "George Bush: 'God Told Me to End the Tyranny in Iraq.'" *Guardian*, October 7, 2005. https://www.theguardian.com/world/2005/oct/07/iraq.usa (May 10, 2023).

Mehta, Jonaki, and Courtney Dorning. "One Man's Outsized Role in Shaping the Supreme Court and Overturning Roe." *NPR*, June 20, 2022. https://www.npr.org/2022/06/30/1108351562/roe-abortion-supreme-court-scotus-law (May 10, 2023).

Methuen, Charlotte. "The English Reformation in Wittenberg: Luther and Melanchthon's Engagement with Religious Change in England 1521–1560." *Reformation & Renaissance Review* 20, no. 3 (2018): 1–40.

Metraux, Daniel. "The Aum Shinrikyo Incident, Revision of the Religious Corporation Law and the Debate over the Separation of Church and State in Contemporary Japan." Paper presented at Japan Seminar, Washington, DC, April 26, 1996.

Miller, Roy Andrew. *Japan's Modern Myth*. New York: Weatherhill, 1982.

Ministry of Education. *"Ippan no kyōiku wo shūkyō igai ni tokuritsu sesimuru kunrei no kaishaku ni kansuru ken"* [Notification on the interpretation of the ordinance to distinguish general education from religions], Bureau of Religions and Bureau of General Educational Affairs Notification No. 102. Issued December 2, 1932. In *Meiji igo shūkyō kankei hōrei ruisan* [Collection of religion-related laws and ordinances since the Meiji era], edited by the Ministry of Education, 948. Tokyo: Daiichihoki Shuppan, 1968.

Ministry of Home Affairs. Shrine Board. *Jinja hongi* [Principles of the shrine]. Tokyo: Japanese Government Printing Bureau, 1944.

Minowa, Kenryō. "Gendai Nihon bukkyo no tokuchō" [Characteristics of contemporary Japanese Buddhism]. *Bulletin of the Faculty of Letters of Aichi Gakuin University* 38 (2008): 345–64.

Misra, Amadendu. "Hindu Nationalism and Muslim Minority Rights in India." *International Journal on Minority and Group Rights* 7, no. 1 (2000): 1–18. http://www.jstor.org/stable/24675146 (May 15, 2023).

Miyazawa, Toshiyoshi. *Kenpō kaisei* [Constitutional revision]. Tokyo: Yuhikaku Publishing, 1956.

Mueller, Dennis C. "The State and Religion." *Review of Social Economy* 71, no. 1 (2013): 1–19. https://doi.org/10.1080/00346764.2012.681115 (May 15, 2023).

Murakami, Shigeyoshi. *Gendai shūkyō to seiji* [Contemporary religions and politics]. Tokyo: University of Tokyo Press, 1978.

Murakami, Shigeyoshi. *Kokka Shinto* [State Shinto]. Tokyo: Iwanami Shoten, 1970.

Najmabadi, Shannon. "Gov. Greg Abbott Signs into Law One of Nation's Strictest Abortion Measures, Banning Procedure as Early as Six Weeks into a Pregnancy." *Texas Tribune*, May 19, 2021. https://www.texastribune.org/2021/05/18/texas-heartbeat-bill-abortions-law/ (May 10, 2023).

Nakano, Minoru. *Shūkyō to seiji* [Religion and politics]. Tokyo: Shinhyoron Publishing, 1998.

Nakano, Tsuyoshi. *Sengo Nihon no shūkyō to seiji* [Religion and politics in postwar Japan]. Tokyo: Taimeido, 2003.

Nakazawa, Shunsuke. *Chian Ijihō* [The Maintenance of Public Order Law]. Tokyo: Chuokoron-shinsha, 2012.

Nichiren Shōshū Head Temple. *Nichiren Shōshū intatsu* [Nichiren Shōshū official notification], no. 2328. Issued October 10, 1942. Cited in *Dai-Nihiren* (November 1942): 1.

Nichiren. "Shuju onfurumai gosho" [The actions of the votary of the Lotus Sutra]. Written 1276. In *Nichiren Daishōnin gosho zenshū* [Collection of literature of Nichiren], edited by the Committee for Publishing the New Collection of Literature of Nichiren, 1225–47. Tokyo: Sōka Gakkai, 2021.

Noda, Yoshiyuki. *Introduction to Japanese Law.* Tokyo: University of Tokyo Press, 1976.

O'Brien, David. *To Dream of Dreams: Religious Freedom and Constitutional Politics in Postwar Japan.* Honolulu: University of Hawaii Press, 1996.

Ogino, Fujio. *Shisō kenji* [Thought prosecutors]. Tokyo: Iwanami Shoten, 2000.

Oginoj, Fujio. *Tokkō keisatsu* [Special higher police]. Tokyo: Iwanami Shoten, 2012.

Oh, Gyeong-seob, Hong Suk-hoon, Hong Jea-hwan, Jeong Eun-mee, and Yee Ji-sun. *White Paper on Human Rights in North Korea 2021*. Seoul: Korea Institute for National Unification, 2021. https://www.kinu.or.kr/main/eng (May 5, 2023).

Paine, Thomas. *Common Sense*. Pamphlet. 1776. https://oll.libertyfund.org/page/1776-paine-common-sense-pamphlet (May 5, 2023).

Paramore, Kiri. "Premodern Secularism." *Japan Review* 30 (2017): 21–37.

Percival, Kelly. "Religion Must Not Substitute Science in the Abortion Debate." *Brennan Center for Justice at NYU Law*, November 5, 2021. https://www.brennancenter.org/our-work/analysis-opinion/religion-must-not-substitute-science-abortion-debate (May 10, 2023).

Pew Research Center. "Religious Groups Issue Statements on War with Iraq." Compiled by Religion News Service, March 19, 2003. https://www.pewresearch.org/religion/2003/03/19/publicationpage-aspxid616/ (May 10, 2023).

Pflüger, Friedbert. "Human Rights Unbound: Carter's Human Rights Policy Reassessed." *Presidential Studies Quarterly* 19, no. 4 (1989): 705–16. http://www.jstor.org/stable/27550568 (May 15, 2023).

Proclamation Defining Terms for Japanese Surrender (Potsdam Declaration). Issued July 26, 1945. https://history.state.gov/historicaldocuments/frus1945Berlinv02/d1382 (May 2, 2023).

PRRI Staff. "The American Religious Landscape in 2020." *PRRI*, July 8, 2021. https://www.prri.org/research/2020-census-of-american-religion/ (May 5, 2023).

Putin, Vladimir. "Address by the President of the Russian Federation." *Official Internet Resources of the President of Russia*, February 21, 2022. http://en.kremlin.ru/events/president/news/67828 (May 11, 2023).

Putin, Vladimir. "Address by the President of the Russian Federation." *Official Internet Resources of the President of Russia*, February 24, 2022. http://en.kremlin.ru/events/president/news/67843 (May 11, 2023).

Putin, Vladimir. "'Those Storms Will Contribute to Russia's Glory': Putin Quotes National Hero to Packed Stadium." (Speech), *NBC News*, March 19, 2022. https://www.nbcnews.com/video/at-huge-rally-putin-uses-bible-and-russian-history-to-justify-ukraine-invasion-135721541797 (May 11, 2023).

Ramachandran, Sudha. "Hindutva Violence in India: Trends and Implications." *Counter Terrorist Trends and Analyses* 12, no. 4 (2020): 15–20. https://www.jstor.org/stable/26918077.

Religion and Public Life. "Cult of Emperor." N.d. https://rpl.hds.harvard.edu/faq/cult-emperor (May 11, 2023).

Reuters. "Abortion Access in a Post-Roe America." *Reuters Graphics*, June 24, 2022. https://graphics.reuters.com/USA-ABORTION/GRAPHIC/zgpomdbeopd/index.html (May 10, 2023).

Rhodes, Christopher. "The Federalist Society: Architects of the American Dystopia." *Al Jazeera*, June 29, 2022. https://www.aljazeera.com/opinions/2022/6/29/the-federalist-society-architects-of-the-american-dystopia (May 10, 2023).

Rock, Stephen. *Faith and Foreign Policy*. London: Bloomsbury Publishing, 2011.

Russian Government. "National Security Concept of the Russian Federation." *Medzinárodné Otázky* 9, no. 3 (2000): 112. http://www.jstor.org/stable/44963336 (May 11, 2023).

Saitō, Makoto. "Amerika kakumei to shūkyō" [American Revolution and religion]. In *Amerika to shūkyō* [America and religion], edited by Mori Kōichi, 63–94. Tokyo: Japan Institute of International Affairs, 1997.

Satō, Hiroo. *Kami, hotoke, ōken no chūsē* [Medieval period of gods, buddhas, and kingship]. Kyoto: Hozokan, 1998.

Satō, Hiroo. *Nihon chūsei no kokka to bukkyō* [State and Buddhism in medieval Japan]. Tokyo: Yoshikawa Kōbunkan, 2010.

Schmitz, David F. and Vanessa Walker. "Jimmy Carter and the Foreign Policy of Human Rights: The Development of a Post-Cold War Foreign Policy." *Diplomatic History* 28, no. 1 (2004): 117. http://www.jstor.org/stable/24914773 (May 15, 2023).

Seager, Richard. *Encountering the Dharma: Daisaku Ikeda, Soka Gakkai, and the Globalization of Buddhist Humanism*. Berkeley: University of California Press, 2006.

Shani, Giorgio. *Religion, Identity and Human Security*. New York: Routledge, 2014.

Shaw, David. "Jimmy Carter's Rise Brought Evangelicalism to the Front Pages." *Los Angeles Times*, December 28, 1983.

Shimazono, Susumu. *Gendai kyūsai shūkyō-ron* [A study of modern salvation religion]. Tokyo: Seikyusha, 1992.

Shin, Eun Hee. "The Sociopolitical Organism: The Religious Dimensions of Juche Philosophy." In *Religions of Korea in Practice,* edited by Robert E. Buswell, 517–33. Princeton: Princeton University Press, 2018.

Shin, Gerry, and Anant Gupta. "Religious Clashes Across India Spark Fears of Further Violence." *Washington Post*, April 20, 2022. https://www.washingtonpost.com/world/2022/04/20/india-hindu-muslim-communal-violence/ (May 5, 2023).

Sodei, Rinjirō, comp. and trans. *Yoshida Shigeru—MacArthur ōfuku shokanshū [1945–1951]* [Collection of correspondences between Yoshida Shigeru and MacArthur]. Tokyo: Hosei University Press, 2000.

State-War-Navy Coordinating Committee of the US Government. *Reform of the Japanese Government System*, January 7, 1946. https://history.state.gov/historicaldocuments/frus1946v08/d116 (May 2, 2023).

Steding, William. *Presidential Faith and Foreign Policy*. London: Palgrave Macmillan, 2014.

Stewart, Katherine. "How the Christian Right Took over the Judiciary and Changed America." *Guardian*, June 25, 2022. https://www.theguardian.com/world/2022/jun/25/roe-v-wade-abortion-christian-right-america (May 10, 2023).

Stolberg, Sheryl Gay. "Thomas's Concurring Opinion Raises Questions About What Rights Might Be Next." *New York Times*, June 24, 2022. https://www.nytimes.com/2022/06/24/us/clarence-thomas-roe-griswold-lawrence-obergefell.html (May 10, 2023).

Takeuchi, Keiichi. *Modern Japanese Geography: An Intellectual History*. [In Japanese.] Tokyo: Kokon Shoin, 2000.

Tamamuro, Fumio. *Edo bakufu no shūkyō tōsei* [Edo feudal government's religious control]. Tokyo: Hyoronsha, 1987.

Taylor, Lily Ross. "The Cult of Alexander at Alexandria." *Classical Philology* 22, no. 2 (April 1927): 162–69. http://www.jstor.org/stable/263514 (May 11, 2023)

Texas Freedom Network. "Group Prepares to Anoint Greg Abbott as Religious Right's Favored Candidate in Texas Governor's Race." *Texas Freedom Network Blog*, March 11, 2014. https://tfn.org/group-prepares-to-anoint-greg-abbott-as-religious-rights-favored-candidate-in-texas-governors-race/ (May 10, 2023).

Thames, Knox. "Putin's Unholy War." *Atlantic Council: UkraineAlert* (blog), April 22, 2022. https://www.atlanticcouncil.org/blogs/ukrainealert/putins-unholy-war/ (May 11, 2023).

Thomas, Clarence. "Justice Thomas' Concurring Opinion on Thomas E. Dobbs, State Health Officer of the Mississippi Department of Health, et al.,

Petitioners v. Jackson Women's Health Organization, et al." 597 US (2022), no. 19-1392, June 24, 2022, *Supreme Court of Justice of the United States syllabus*, October Term 2021. https://www.supremecourt.gov/opinions/21pdf/19-1392_6j37.pdf (May 10, 2023).

Tocqueville, Alexis de. *Democracy in America.* Vol. 1. Translated by Henry Reeve. Electric edition. Charlottesville: University of Virginia, 1997. https://xroads.virginia.edu/~Hyper/DETOC/1_ch17.htm (May 15, 2023).

Tokugawa Government. "Shūmon Torishimari Kisoku" [Sect Control Regulations]. Issued 1613. In *Nihon shūkyō zenshi* [History of Japanese religions], Vol. 4, edited by Hiyane Antei, 134–36. Tokyo: Kyobunkan, 1942.

Torrance, David. *The Relationship Between Church and State in the United Kingdom*. London: House of Commons Library, 2021.

Turnbull, Stephen. *Japanese Warrior Monks AD 949–1603*. New York: Bloomsbury Publishing, 2012.

United Methodist Communications. "Church Executive Urges Bush Not to Attack Iraq." Press release, September 3, 2002. https://archive.wfn.org/2002/09/msg00033.html (May 10, 2023).

United Nations General Assembly. *Report of the Special Rapporteur to the 76th session of the General Assembly: On the Situation of Human Rights in the Democratic People's Republic of Korea*, A/76/392. October 8, 2021. https://www.ohchr.org/en/documents/country-reports/a76392-report-special-rapporteur-76th-session-general-assembly (May 5, 2023).

United Nations Human Rights Council. *Promoting Accountability in the Democratic People's Republic of Korea: Report of the United Nations High Commissioner for Human Rights*, A/HR/46/52. January 11, 2021. https://digitallibrary.un.org/record/3898922 (May 5, 2023).

United Nations Human Rights Council. *Report of the Detailed Findings of the Commission of Inquiry on Human Rights in the Democratic People's Republic of Korea*, A/HR/25/CRP. February 7, 2014. https://www.ohchr.org/en/hr-bodies/hrc/co-idprk/reportofthe-commissionof-inquiry-dprk (May 5, 2023).

US Congress. *Congressional Record*, February 10, 2022, vol. 168, issue 27. https://www.govinfo.gov/app/details/CREC-2022-02-10 (May 11, 2023).

US Department of State. *2021 Report on International Religious Freedom: Democratic People's Republic of Korea (DPRK)*. Office of International Religious Freedom, June 2, 2021. https://www.state.gov/reports/2021-report-on-international-religious-freedom/north-korea/ (May 5, 2023).

US Department of State. *World Military Expenditures and Arms Transfers 2021.* December 31, 2021. https://www.state.gov/world-military-expenditures-and-arms-transfers-2021-edition/ (May 5, 2023).

Volochinsky, Brigitte P. “The Bush Presidency: Undermining the Separation Between Church and State.” Inquiries Journal 2, no. 7 (2010). http://www.inquiriesjournal.com/articles/266/the-bush-presidency-undermining-the-separation-between-church-and-state (May 10, 2023).

Volz, Carl A. *The Medieval Church: From the Dawn of the Middle Ages to the Eve of the Reformation*. Nashville: Abingdon Press, 2011.

Vulliamy, Ed. “Iraq War ‘Unjustifiable’ Says Bush’s Church Head.” *Guardian*, October 20, 2002. https://www.theguardian.com/world/2002/oct/20/usa.iraq (May 10, 2023).

Wallis, Jim. “Dangerous Religion: George W. Bush’s Theology of Empire.” *Mississippi Review* 32, no. 3 (2004): 60–72. http://www.jstor.org/stable/20132445.

Walters, Philip. “The Russian Orthodox Church and the Soviet State.” *The Annals of the American Academy of Political and Social Science* 483 (1986): 135–45. http://www.jstor.org/stable/1045546 (May 5, 2023).

Weber, Max. *The Sociology of Religion*, translated by Ephraim Fischoff. Boston: Beacon Press, 1964.

Whitehouse, Sheldon. “The Third Federalist Society.” Speech presented March 27, 2019. https://www.whitehouse.senate.gov/news/speeches/the-third-federalist-society (May 10, 2023).

Wilson, John, and Donald Drakeman. *Church and State in American History: Key Documents, Decisions, and Commentary from Five Centuries*. Oxfordshire: Routledge, 2019.

Wilson, John. “Religion and Revolution in American History.” *Journal of Interdisciplinary History* 23, no. 3 (1993): 597–613. https://doi.org/10.2307/206104 (May 15, 2023).

Witte Jr., J., and M. C. Green, eds. *Religion and Human Rights: An Introduction*. New York: Oxford University Press, 2011.

Wolferen, Karel. “America and Japan: 50 Years Later; An Economic Pearl Harbor?” *New York Times*, December 2, 1991. https://www.nytimes.com/1991/12/02/opinion/america-and-japan-50-year-later-an-economic-pearl-harbor.html (May 3, 2023).

Wolferen, Karel. *The Enigma of Japanese Power*. Tokyo: Charles E. Tuttle Co., 1993.

Yamaguchi, Natsuo. “Regular Press Briefing by the Representative of Kōmeitō.” July 26, 2022, video of briefing. https://www.youtube.com/watch?v=J8U0G15_tA4 (May 3, 2023)

Index

About the Author

Tokihisa (Andy) Sumimoto is a lecturer in the Graduate School of Intercultural Communication, Rikkyo University, Tokyo, Japan, also known as St. Paul's University, as well as in the Faculty of Foreign Studies, Kanda University of International Studies, and at Kunitachi College of Music. He received his MIA from Columbia University School of International and Public Affairs and his PhD from Soka University, where he was a visiting scholar at the Peace Research Institute.